Taking Charge of My Mind & Body

A Girls' Guide to Outsmarting Alcohol, Drug, Smoking, and Eating Problems

GLADYS FOLKERS, M.A., AND JEANNE ENGELMANN

Free Spirit ®

PUBLISHING

The stories and quotations in this book are about and by real girls and young women, but their names have been changed to protect their privacy.

The authors gratefully acknowledge the work of young poet, Amy Cullen, who wrote "Imagine a Young Woman" on page viii. Her poem has been reprinted with her permission.

Library of Congress Cataloging-in-Publication Data

Folkers, Gladys. 1947–
   Taking charge of my mind & body : a girls' guide to outsmarting alcohol, drug, smoking, and eating problems / Gladys Folkers and Jeanne Engelmann.
      p.   cm.
   Includes bibliographical references and index.
   Summary: Offers advice, with quotes from teenagers, on making appropriate choices about using alcohol and other drugs, smoking, dealing with body image and eating disorders, and other adolescent concerns.
   ISBN 1-57542-015-5
   1. Teenage girls—Health and hygiene—Juvenile literature. 2. Teenage girls—Mental health—Juvenile literature. 3. Substance abuse—Juvenile literature. 4. Eating disorders—Juvenile literature. [1. Conduct of life. 2. Substance abuse. 3. Eating disorders. 4. Health.] I. Engelmann, Jeanne. II. Title.
   RA777.25.F65   1997   96-46732
   613'.04243—dc21   CIP
                                                                  AC

Edited by Pamela Espeland and Elizabeth Verdick
Cover design by Circus Design
Illustrations by Marie Olofsdotter
Index compiled by Eileen Quam and Theresa Wolner

NOTE: The chart on page 15, "Identifying Drugs and Their Effects," is a basic overview only. It is not designed as a complete reference to all aspects of drug types, effects, appearances, and uses. If you need specific information in an emergency situation, call your doctor, your local poison control center, or 911.

10 9 8 7 6 5 4 3 2 1

Printed in the United States of America

Free Spirit Publishing Inc.
400 First Avenue North, Suite 616
Minneapolis, MN 55401-1730
(612) 338-2068
help4kids@freespirit.com

This book is dedicated
to girls all over the world
who struggle each day
to survive,
to be somebody,
to soar.
May you all succeed.

Acknowledgments

We would like to thank a host of people who helped by sharing their stories, ideas, expertise, concerns, gripes, and wise counsel. Special thanks to all the girls on our editorial review board and those who shared bits and pieces of their lives with us: the girls in the groups we spoke with; the girls who shared their own personal stories; the girls who read, reviewed, and commented on the manuscript, including our daughters Kim, Michelle, Jali, and Kate; and the many girls who shared their thoughts by answering our survey questions.

Thanks, too, to the many professionals who work every day with girls and who so willingly shared their insights with us. Special thanks to Kay Provine, Barbara Weiner, Mary Ellen Connolly, and Beth Milligan for their ongoing support and wise counsel. We are grateful to staff members at Minnetonka Middle School East and High School; the Eating Disorders Institute, Methodist Hospital; Alfred Adler Institute of Minnesota; the Highview Alternative and the Middle Level Alternative Programs in Robbinsdale; and to the principals and faculty of the schools who facilitated our survey distribution. Our special thanks to the many individuals who helped with information, reviewing, and guidance and to our families for their help and patience.

Contents

Imagine a Young Woman
by Amy Cullen, 15

Imagine a young woman . . .
Who isn't afraid to stand up for what she believes,
Who can be intelligent and beautiful,
Who asks out the guys she likes,
Who doesn't have to gossip to have things to talk about,
Who doesn't always have to have a boyfriend,
Who can talk with her parents and friends without anger,
Who can balance her studies with chores and fun,
Who wants to enter a field that's considered
    "for men only,"
Who isn't afraid to be herself,
Who has control over her emotions and can decide if
    she's going to be sad, angry, or happy,
Who has enough self-confidence to save herself until
    she's married,
Who isn't afraid of people or things that are different,
Who doesn't have to put others down in order to
    feel okay,
Who, when she sees a wrong, does what she can to
    make it right,
Who empathizes with others,
Who participates in sports, even if those sports are
    dominated by males,
Who is proud of her heritage, sex, religion, and sexual
    identity,
Who isn't afraid to say "no,"
Who smiles true smiles,
Who thinks before she speaks,
Who speaks with a free spirit.
Imagine this young woman as the person you want to be.

Introduction

Crispy Fried, or Clear and Sure?

What happens to you when you get hooked on drugs, smoke heavily, or drink too much? What happens if you eat too much or too little, or diet all the time and exercise too much? You might end up with Crispy Fried Brains and a Crispy Fried Body.

You won't find "Crispy Fried" in the dictionary, so here's a working definition for you:

crispy fried: unable to think clearly; having a slow reaction time and a fuzzy, confused sense of reality; feeling tired, weak, or burned-out; unable to understand problems, choose solutions, and follow through; unable to take charge of one's life.

It's *your* mind, and it's *your* body. You have the power to choose the best way to care for both. As a teenager, it's important to have all of your wits about you in order to understand yourself and your surroundings, choose actions that will help you to be successful in any situation,

"I didn't like the feeling drugs gave me. I thought using them was stupid. I saw how drugs crispy fried my friends. What's good about not using? Not feeling crispy fried around the edges."

Carmen, 16

1

and take steps to meet your goals—hard to do when you're crispy fried. But when you're confident and healthy, and when you're strong in mind, body, and spirit, you'll have a better chance of overcoming obstacles and achieving personal success.

What obstacles? Despite the fact that we've come pretty far, the girls and young women of today are still marching uphill against odds that boys don't necessarily face. For example, girls sometimes struggle more with shame and poor self-esteem. More girls than boys experience depression and physical, sexual, and emotional abuse. More girls than boys struggle with eating disorders. And social and cultural trends—ideas made popular by music, television, and movies—continue to portray girls and women as not-very-important objects.

Girls and women also continue to carry most of the responsibility for sexual relationships, including childrearing. If you aren't clear-headed, you might make choices that will affect you in a negative way now and for a lifetime. For example, if you drink too much one time, at one party, you may be vulnerable to sexual activity that's either unwanted or unprotected. Having sex one time, at one party, may be all it takes to become pregnant or to get a sexually transmitted disease. One poor choice about drinking or drugs could change your life forever.

Want to beat those odds? By being clear and sure, you'll increase your ability to:

- think for yourself,
- make good decisions, and
- take positive action to protect yourself and your future.

This goes for you *and* your friends. You've probably seen your friends or other girls you know smoking, drinking, using drugs, or eating in unhealthy ways. Girls and young women are doing these things more than ever before. The good news is you can find help for yourself and your friends.

Seven Reasons to Worry

Why should you care about alcohol and other drug use, smoking, or eating problems? Here are seven important reasons:

1. Abuse

When using leads to abusing alcohol, drugs, cigarettes, and/or food, you place yourself at a much higher risk for trouble in life, including addiction.

2. Addiction

Addiction happens when you're unable to stop using even though problems from your drug use are piling up. As a teen, you're in danger of getting hooked for several reasons. For example, you may be more likely to take risks, or you may not be aware of the signs of addiction.

3

3. Poor Grades

Drinking, using drugs, and abusing food can seriously hurt your ability to think clearly and focus. Which can seriously ruin your grades and school performance. Which can negatively affect your future career and life goals.

4. Lifetime Patterns

The eating, drinking, smoking, and drug use patterns you adopt now are likely to follow you through your life. If you learn now to cope with feelings of sadness, frustration, anger, or boredom by using drugs, for instance, you'll probably carry that coping method with you into, and throughout, your adult life.

5. Life Problems

When you're addicted to alcohol and other drugs, you're more likely to have problems with being sick, poor, a victim of violence and accidents, or involved in crime. People who have eating disorders face a variety of serious health problems, which can eventually lead to an early death.

6. Children with Problems

Girls and women who drink, smoke, use drugs, or have an eating disorder during pregnancy can seriously harm the health of their babies.

7. Gateway to More Use

Marijuana, alcohol, nicotine, and inhalants are some-times called "gateway" drugs. This means they are the "gates" you might pass through to use of other, more dangerous drugs (cocaine, speed, crack, heroin, etc.). Some teens think that drinking a beer or smoking pot is harmless, and they give it a try. Having tried those drugs sometimes makes it easier and more tempting to try drugs that are even more hazardous.

The Role of Feelings and Mistaken Beliefs

Drinking. Drugs. Smoking. Eating disorders. What's common in all of these problems? Two things: *feelings* and *mistaken beliefs*.

Feelings are often confusing to people of all ages. Am I angry or hurt? Why am I feeling embarrassed? Did I do something stupid, or is this situation weird? Am I sad or mad? When you're feeling something strongly and aren't sure what it's all about, you might easily discover that a beer, a smoke, or a package of Oreos can make you feel better (temporarily, that is). On the other hand, if you know it's fine to feel the way you do, then you'll be less likely to drink, take drugs, smoke, or eat to deal with your feelings.

According to Alfred Adler, a famous psychiatrist who lived from 1870–1937, and whose ideas are still changing lives today, mistaken beliefs often play a role in leading people of all ages into problem behavior. *Mistaken* means inaccurate, misguided, or confused. *Beliefs* are convictions, opinions, or ideas. Mistaken beliefs are formed when we're very young—before age six. We observe a situation and then interpret it. Before age six, we don't have the mental ability to interpret correctly, so we come up with some beliefs that are mistaken. Sometimes our mistaken beliefs are connected to smoking, bad eating habits, and using alcohol and other drugs. When you become aware of some of your mistaken beliefs, and find ways to change them, you can be more successful in your day-to-day living.

If you haven't started drinking, using drugs, smoking, or fixating on food and your body, continue strengthening your decision to live free of those problems. But if you're already experimenting with smoking and using, or if you think you might have a problem with eating, you can do something about it. Even if you've been struggling with one or more of these issues for some time, it's not too late to get help. Whatever your situation is, you can try these steps:

1. Know you're not bad for doing these things and that your feelings are okay.
2. Realize the reasons behind your choice.
3. Choose differently.

You may say, "Oh, sure, like I have any choice at all in anything I do." The fact is, you *always* have a choice. Chances are that, in any situation, you probably have several possible choices. It's our hope that by reading this book you'll learn to assume that you always have options in any situation, and that you'll take the time to choose what's right for you. You have the power to choose well.

About This Book

This book explores:

- problems that alcohol and drug use, smoking, and eating disorders can create for you,
- feelings and mistaken beliefs that tempt you to use substances and/or to have problems with food, and
- ways to change your thinking and to make different choices about how you treat your mind and body.

The first three parts of this book are about alcohol and other drugs, smoking, and eating disorders. You'll learn about what it's really like to face these problems, the effects these problems can have on your life, what other girls have gone through, and what to do if you need help. There's a mix of quotes and stories by real girls, steps you can take to help yourself or a friend, fast facts that might inform and even surprise you, and reality checks for fine-tuning your thinking.

In each part, you'll also find suggestions for where to go for help. Realize that you don't have to face your problems alone. There are many people you can reach out to, including a parent, a teacher, a counselor, a doctor, or other expert. We've provided numbers for hotlines and information lines you can call, plus addresses for sites on the World Wide Web for readers who have access to a computer and the Internet. We've screened these Web sites to make sure they're positive sources of information and support. Because Web sites come and go, and change very quickly, we can't promise that everything we say about them will still be current and accurate when you read this book. But our suggestions should give you a start in the right direction.

The last part of the book describes steps for positive change. You'll figure out if your thinking is clear and sure, or mistaken. You'll find out how to strengthen the ways you relate to yourself and to others. And you'll learn to think through how you handle your feelings. Most importantly, you'll learn some strategies for taking charge of your life—strategies that you can use right away and for a lifetime.

So . . . crispy fried, or clear and sure? It's up to you. The choices you make today will affect you today, tomorrow, and possibly for as long as you live. We hope this book helps you to choose what you take into your body and to make those choices in a careful, thoughtful way. We want you to claim yourself as a valuable, successful, terrific person who intends to be somebody. A confident, healthy, clear, sure girl.

*"Be sure
that if you drink
or use drugs
you know why you're
doing it.*

> *If you're doing it
> to feel better,
> don't.*

*Just look at people
who are using
and what losers they are."*

Yvonne, 16

Part One

What You Should Know About **Drinking** and *Using Other* **Drugs**

1

Hooked on Alcohol and Other Drugs— What It's Like

"Alcohol kills brain cells."
Ellie, 17

It can start with just one little drink. You're at a party, someone hands you a beer, and you take it, thinking, "Beer's pretty harmless, just one won't hurt." You get used to the taste, the buzz, and you start drinking more at other parties and with your friends. Maybe you start drinking harder stuff later on. Or, something similar happens with other drugs. You start with a joint, then move on to stronger substances like acid, speed, coke, and so on. Is it really such a big deal? The answer is YES! Read on to find out why.

JEANNE: I Just Drank All the Time

I was hooked the moment I had my first drink. Bam. I was maybe 15, doing okay on the surface, but I was lost. I was just wandering around my life looking for a place to be, something to belong to, some way to be important. It was the end of the school year, and a teacher took a group of us to her cabin for the day for a year-end picnic. Those who were old enough to drive and had a car drove the rest of us.

When we got there, my friend and I left the group and found a cabin nearby. It was unlocked so we let ourselves in and rummaged around. I opened a cabinet, and there was a full bottle of gin.

I didn't pause or think. I grabbed it, found some glasses, and poured. I know now that what happened next was pretty typical. My friend stopped after a shot or two. I drank until I couldn't stand up. My head felt like it was spinning every time I glanced around the room, making me feel sick. I was so drunk that the other kids hid me for the afternoon and then made sure I got loaded into one of the cars being driven by a classmate. I really embarrassed myself in front of everyone, throwing up all over the car a couple times before getting home.

Luckily, my mother wasn't home. My friend got me to my room without anyone else in the family knowing. Then she stayed around until my mom got there. My friend lied to my mother that I was sick with the flu and sleeping. That bought me enough time to sleep it off, sober up, and get through the incident without my family figuring it out.

What's important about this story is that I drank the first time until I was drunk, and that's how I drank every time afterward. From that day on, I drank to the exclusion of every other activity. Two years later, by the time I was ready to graduate from high school, I was a full-blown alcoholic with no ability to reign it back in. I was so depressed I could barely move.

I was having blackouts, not able to remember what I did when drunk, so I was failing courses. I'd study for tests, but I drank in my room while studying. The next morning, I'd come to a test and just draw a complete blank, like I'd never seen the stuff before in my life.

Well, I got to the point where I couldn't function. I just drank all the time. My parents finally got help from the local mental health center and sent me off to a treatment center, where I stayed for what seemed like forever. I think it will take me the rest of my life to sort out everything that's happened to me because of my drinking. Some of it's okay, because treatment helped me figure out how to live in better ways.

But I do feel like I never had a teenage life, a kid life. It's just gone. The time is past. I hear others talk about the great, tight friends they made in high school, and how the good grades they got helped them get into the colleges they wanted, and the fun times they had. Well, I can't relate. It just didn't happen like that for me. My only real friend was alcohol.

And you know what bugs me the most? It just happened. I didn't know a thing about alcohol or other drug use. I didn't realize what I was doing, or why, or what was happening. All I really knew was that the stuff in the bottle made me feel better. I wish I could have figured out somehow that I was in trouble and needed a specific kind of help before I got beyond the point of no return.

I know it doesn't happen like this for everyone, but for some of us, no matter how young we are, drinking and drugs grab us and hold on until the life is squeezed out of us. When the hold is broken, we can only wonder what we would have been like if none of that had happened.

What's the Harm?

"I would say that there's no good reason to use drugs or alcohol. There are better, healthier ways to have fun."
Jessye, 15

Girls have said they drank or used just because it was there, because they hadn't really thought it through, or they told themselves, "Just one won't hurt." In other words, many girls and young women ended up using because they hadn't realized the effects, or dangers, of these substances.

But drinking and using other drugs is known to cause a lot of harm to people. For example, heavy marijuana use can create problems in your thinking and ability to function. Alcohol use also impairs your thinking, plus your judgment—leaving you vulnerable to accidents, unsafe decisions about sex, and other types of risks.

Fast Facts

Alcohol is the most destructive drug among teens who use drugs:

- It's the drug teens use first, at the earliest age.
- 8,000 young people die each year in car accidents that involve alcohol use.
- Alcohol is involved in most violent deaths suffered by teenagers, and its use is closely linked to teen suicide.
- Alcohol leads young people to take greater risks in all areas of their lives.
- Students with grades of D and F drink three times as much as those who earn A's.

Alcohol and pot are known as "gateway" drugs, because—for many people—they are a "gate" to use of other, harder drugs. In other words, a girl might get drunk or high on pot a few times; she's taken the risk, broken the law, and maybe figures the experience was no big deal. Next time, she might be tempted to try something even more risky (coke, crack, heroin, etc.). Consider this statistic: Teens who drink alcohol are around 50 times more likely to use cocaine. And this one: Young people who smoke pot are about 85 times more likely to use cocaine. So, if you think these gateway drugs are harmless, you're wrong.

Today, many kinds of hard drugs are more accessible to young people than ever before. It may be relatively easy for you to find someone in your school or neighborhood who's dealing drugs like cocaine, uppers, downers, heroin, crack, or hallucinogens (like acid or ecstasy). These kinds of drugs can be very addictive and dangerous, *even if used just once.* If someone comes up to you and offers you a drug, it's important to know exactly what it is and what its effects are. The chart on page 15 can help you identify certain drugs, how they're taken, and what they do to your mind and body.

Fast Facts

- When THC (the primary active chemical in pot) was given to lab rats, it caused their brains to look like those of animals in old age.

- The effects of pot can last up to three days, decreasing your memory and coordination.

- Glue or other inhalants enter your bloodstream and go through your body in seconds. Sniffing large amounts can cause a heart attack.

- People have died from the "natural" ingredients in the drug herbal X.

- After taking a drug like heroin, your body chemistry can start to change to adapt to the presence of the drug—making your body crave more.

- If you buy a bag of coke from a dealer, chances are the white powder you're getting is mixed with a substance like talcum powder, baking soda, or even poisonous household cleaners.

- Speed is very habit-forming. Heavy use can cause confusion, paranoia, convulsions, and even brain damage.

- Taking LSD, PCP, or ecstasy can cause a "bad trip," which might last up to 12 hours.

- Heroin users often shoot up with needles, increasing their chances of getting AIDS, hepatitis, or blood poisoning.

Identifying Drugs and Their Effects

Name of Drug	What It Looks Like	How It's Taken	Effects
Amphetamines and methamphetamines (speed, crank, meth, crystal)	Tablet/capsule	Snorted, smoked, or injected	Nervousness, overexcitement
Barbiturates (downers)	Tablet/capsule	Swallowed	Slowed-down brain and body
Cocaine (coke, snow, blow, flake)	White powder	Snorted, smoked (freebasing), or injected	Increased energy, followed by a "crash"
Crack (rock cocaine)	Rocks or chunks	Smoked through a crack pipe	Increased energy, followed by a "crash"
Heroin (smack, horse, junk, H, redrum)	Powder ranging from white to brown in color	Snorted, smoked, or injected (mainlining)	Feeling of well-being, followed by slowed heart rate, nausea, drowsiness, and cravings for more heroin
Inhalants (poppers, rush, laughing gas)	Various forms (glue, lighter fluid, hair spray, cleaning products)	Sniffed or "huffed" from bottles or soaked cloths	A high that lasts a few minutes or up to an hour, decreased oxygen to the brain
Lysergic acid diethylamide (LSD, acid, microdot)	Tablet/capsule, small squares of paper	Swallowed	Hallucinations, twisted reality, loss of control over body and mind
Marijuana (pot, grass, joint, weed, reefer, ganja—in a stronger form it's hashish)	Dried leaves (hashish is a resin; usually comes in a chunk)	Smoked	A dream-like state, distorted sense of time, panic, food cravings ("munchies")
MDMA (ecstasy, adam)	Tablet (various sizes and colors)	Swallowed, or crushed and snorted	Hallucinations, overstimulation, illusions
Methaqualone (quaaludes, ludes)	Tablet	Swallowed	Disorientation, slurred speech
Mushrooms (magic mushrooms, shrooms)	Dried mushrooms	Eaten	Hallucinations, twisted reality
Phencyclidine (PCP, angel dust)	Tablet/capsule, white powder, liquid	Swallowed, smoked, or injected	Hallucinations, twisted reality, loss of control over body and mind
Tranquilizers (downers)	Tablet/capsule	Swallowed	Disorientation, slurred speech

TAKING CHARGE OF MY MIND & BODY, copyright © 1997 by Gladys Folkers and Jeanne Engelmann, Free Spirit Publishing Inc. This page may be photocopied.

Drinking Games

"**C**hugging," "slamming," "doing beer bongs." Otherwise known as binge drinking, or gulping drinks, these activities have recently become more common. So have drinking games like "Quarters." In the past, males played these games more often than females. But over the last decade, those numbers have been evening out.

Drinking games and binge drinking often involve downing a shot of hard liquor or gulping a bottle/can of beer without stopping. Young people die every year from alcohol poisoning due to drinking too fast for the body to process the alcohol and clear it from the system. Risky drinking games often happen at keg parties, at homes where parents are gone for the weekend, and at lake cabins and parks.

A common result of these games is you consume so much alcohol in a short period that you end up getting drunk much faster. You quickly lose control of your body and mind. In other words, you become bombed, toasted, wasted, loaded, hammered, smashed, ripped, blitzed, sloshed, tanked, blasted, or plastered. Would you want to be described this way? Would you want this to happen to someone you care about?

"I had to experience chugging for myself to believe the effects. And I only had to do it once to realize that it's a scary experience and isn't worth it."
Priscilla, 15

Fast Facts

- On average, it takes 60 minutes to process 1/2 ounce of pure alcohol. 1/2 ounce of alcohol is the same as a 12-ounce bottle of beer, a 5-ounce glass of wine, or a 1 1/2 ounce shot of liquor.

- When given the same amount of alcohol, males and females of the same weight are affected differently. Females quickly develop higher blood-alcohol levels because they produce less of a certain enzyme that helps absorb alcohol in the stomach. When less alcohol is broken down in the stomach, more of it reaches the bloodstream. The result is that women and girls generally get drunk more quickly.

Take into account that you're probably smaller and weigh less than many of the boys you play drinking games with. That means if you're drinking the same amount as they are, it's very likely that much more alcohol is reaching your bloodstream. Add to that the fact that the guys around you naturally produce more of an enzyme that helps break down alcohol in the stomach (see "Fast Facts" above), and the result is you're getting drunk a lot faster. So it's extremely dangerous for you and your female friends to play drinking games. The next time someone says, "Hey, chicken, bet you can't drink this straight down," try responding with, "Bet you're right."

But "Everybody's Doing It . . . "

Guess what? Most girls and young women *don't* drink and use other drugs. This may seem hard to believe when you know girls in your circle of friends, your neighborhood, your classes, your school, etc., who drink and do drugs. It's easy to conclude that "Everybody's doing it."

But take a closer look. It's true that many girls and young women are drinking and using. But it's also true that many are not. In 1995–96, PRIDE—an organization dedicated to preventing drug abuse—gave out a questionnaire nationwide to over 60,000 girls in grades 6 through 12. Here's what they found out:

*"I choose
not to use
drugs. I
have goals
set for
myself,
and I don't
want to
screw up."*
Anna, 15

- 50 to 75 percent of girls are *not* drinking.
- 75 percent of girls are *not* smoking pot.
- 90 percent of girls are *not* using other drugs.

So, the next time you're thinking about whether to take a drink or smoke a joint, remember that you have a choice in the matter. If you've learned all you can about what drugs and alcohol can do to you, if you've thought it through ahead of time, it will be easier to make the decision that's right for you.

Reasons Why Some Girls Use

Different girls have different reasons for using alcohol and other drugs. Maybe some of these reasons sound familiar: boredom, feelings of inferiority, curiosity, anger, wanting to feel older or more popular, sadness, the urge to take a risk, confusion, loneliness, the need for attention or acceptance, rebellion, the desire to feel good, for fun, the need to fit in, stress—the list goes on and on. While the reasons are varied, they hold something in common: the normal ups and downs of growing up. The more you know about *why* you're using, and the better you understand your own feelings, the easier it will be to make a different choice.

TANIA: I Never Felt I Could Measure Up

I struggled with grades and schoolwork my whole life. It just didn't come easy to me. I was in some special education classes, but I hated that because I had to be pulled out of regular classes. So here I was, struggling all the way through for just average grades, and what kind of a family do I get? You got it . . . successful high-achievers. All my brothers and sisters made great grades, Dad and Mom both did well in school, and they all had really high expectations of me.

Well, I never felt like I could measure up, and I couldn't find a comfortable niche in my family, like I really belonged and was accepted for who I was. I started to hang around with a group of kids I liked. I think they all felt like I did—misfits who weren't especially good at anything. We all smoked pot, and we drank a lot. I remember the first time I combined the two. I felt sort of high and bad at the same time. I sat in the middle of a party watching a candle flicker, feeling my heart pounding in my ears. I pressed my ears to stop the throbbing and felt giggly and panicky all at the same time.

The more I smoked and drank, the worse my grades got. I started to do things I'd never done before, like staying out later than I was supposed to, cutting classes, and fighting a lot with my family. I started drinking and driving, too, and coming home drunk.

It all got so bad that my parents took me to treatment. Boy, was that a shock. For one thing, I found out I didn't have it so bad. I was in with kids who hadn't been home for months; one kid, Alan, hadn't seen his family for over a year. I spent the first week feeling like I hated the place and everyone in it, and at the same time listening real hard to figure out how to work my way out of my mess. By the time I left, almost two months later, I was hugging everyone in the place while feeling fear rise from the pit of my stomach into my throat as I waited for my parents to pick me up and take me home. I think I was afraid they weren't going to come and get me. And what a relief when they did!

I continued to attend the aftercare meetings when I got out of treatment. Slowly, I made changes. I slipped once and my parents threatened to put me right back into treatment. They set strict limits and set up rules. I worked hard to get better.

Right now, I'm still sober and I'm not using any other drugs. My grades are picking up, and I got a job I really like. It's really been such a struggle, but I feel better. At least for now. I've missed a lot of school, and I want to find some different friends who don't drink and use. It's hard to not use and be around the same friends, but it's really hard to change friends— scary! And when I start feeling bad about something, I'm really tempted to do what I'm used to doing: drinking or smoking pot.

I don't know how long I'll be able to keep away from all of that, but I remind myself that I really do feel better now. I'm even thinking about giving up smoking cigarettes next. But I think I'll just take one thing at a time.

Drinking and other drug use can get all mixed up with adolescent development. For example, the sooner girls go through puberty, the sooner they're likely to drink and smoke, according to a recent Stanford University study. So, if you mature more quickly than your girlfriends, you may be tempted to drink and smoke before they do.

Why? There may be several reasons, all tied up with normal maturation. If you go through puberty early:

- You may feel weird and stressed out because you're ahead of your friends. You may drink or use drugs to ease those feelings.

- You may start hanging out with older kids and start smoking or drinking to prove your sophistication.

- Your hormones change, and that may cause you to have mood swings that you're not used to handling. You may drink to ease or escape from the strange moods.

Even if you go through puberty at about the same time your friends do, you may still feel overwhelmed by all the physical and emotional changes you're going through. Instead of turning to alcohol or other drugs, try finding someone to talk to: a friend, your mom, your sister, a teacher, a counselor, or anyone else who might understand.

Mood Swings

You've heard the jokes about girls and hormones and mood swings. You're probably aware of Premenstrual Syndrome—PMS—and all the humor about girls who turn into "wicked witches" just before getting their periods. Well, hormones are the culprit. And, once

you've gone through puberty, you too may experience the ups and downs that go along with changing hormones.

For many girls and women, hormonal changes and their accompanying mood swings are very normal. Comfortable, no. But normal, yes. When you feel yourself overreacting to things, take time out to do a reality check: Is it really that bad? Does my life truly stink? Will this matter a year or a hundred years from now? Do I really need beer/drugs to deal with this problem? In those out-of-control moments, try to make yourself take a deep breath, think calmly, and find the best solution.

The main thing to keep in mind is that adolescence is a period of time, not a disease. We all go through it. During your teen years, you'll change and experience lots of confusing feelings. You'll have good days and bad. But it's important to learn to deal with your mood swings and feelings in a positive way. Rather than reaching for drugs or alcohol, try comforting yourself in healthy ways: take a hot bath, call a friend, take a walk, do yoga, draw, or buy yourself some flowers.

Fast Facts

Depression and suicide are often linked to use of alcohol and other drugs. Of the more than 60,000 girls in the PRIDE Survey, 4,825 said they thought often or a lot about committing suicide. Of those 4,825 girls:

- 3,042 reported using alcohol,
- 2,187 reported using marijuana,
- 1,206 reported using inhalants, and
- 609 reported using cocaine.

NOTE: If you've had thoughts about suicide, please get help right away! Talk to an adult you trust, and do it today. If that isn't an option for you right now, then look under "Suicide Prevention" in your local phone book. Most cities and many towns have suicide prevention hotlines staffed 24 hours a day, 7 days a week, with people who will listen. Check the "Community Services" section first, if there is one. You can also find hotline listings in the Yellow Pages.

Growing Pains

As a teenager, you may find that your relationships with many different people are intensifying. You're becoming more aware of how people relate to each other, solve problems, and handle feelings and conflicts. You're seeking a sense of who you are in relation to your family, friends, and the world.

This growing sense of your ability to act, to be, to do, and to have an impact on your world can be wonderful. You're discovering your own identity and how you want to live your life. At this time, you're also figuring out how you differ from your family, which values you believe in, and which ones you disagree with.

Family members may be surprised at your new views and interests, and how fast you're growing and changing. It may take some adjustment on everyone's part. Try to keep relating to your family in a healthy way, and help your parents and siblings understand that you still love them. Although your relationships with friends/boyfriends may be deepening, and though you may still be sorting out who you are and how you want to be, it's important to stay connected to your family. This is just one way to move confidently through your teen years.

This is not to say it's going to be easy! As you become more independent of your parents, for example,

"I stopped using drugs because I was burnt out. I couldn't think or concentrate, and it got in the way of my family."
Becky, 17

you'll probably find that it's harder to get along with them. Power struggles can arise, with both sides determined to get their way. When this happens, your natural reaction might be: "They can't tell me what to do," or "I should be able to do what I want," or "They can't make me stay home," or "I'll show them . . . I'll get wasted." Stop and think a moment: Who are you *really* hurting?

LETITIA: It Got So I'd Do Anything Just to Be High

My mother is what I'd call very prim and proper. She's got a good job as a bank receptionist, and she dresses up for it. She doesn't leave the house in the morning without checking herself at least twice in the mirror— you know the type. Well, I'm almost 18 now, but when I was a kid, maybe 11 or 12, I wanted to get her out of my face. So what's the first thing I did? I wore trash. Any old thing I could pick off my bedroom floor, I'd toss on. I'd leave my room a mess, lose things, forget my homework, and all that.

Well, you can guess the next scene here. She yelled, I yelled, and the more she got on me the worse I looked. When that got real boring, I started doing other things I knew she'd hate. Someone offered me a cigarette, I took it. A joint, I smoked it. A beer, I drank it. She could smell it on me, and that led to bigger and better fights.

So, what'd I do? I went on to use other drugs. Someone offered me a line, I snorted it. I dropped acid and some other stuff. It got so I'd do anything just to be high. I mixed up the drugs so I couldn't remember what I'd taken or when.

I don't know exactly what happened, but after a couple years of this, I don't know, I just got tired of it. Bored with it, I guess. Something shifted in me, and I just didn't need to do that stuff anymore. I guess I took an honest look at myself and saw what a mess I was. I remember looking at myself in the mirror and thinking, "Who *is* that?" My hair and face and clothes were a mess. My nose ran all the time, like I always had a cold. By then my mom had stopped fighting with me. I guess she was resigned to me screwing up.

When I got to a point where I wasn't interested in the kids I was hanging with or the parties and same old games, I took a look around me. I was maybe 16 by then. My grades stunk. I hardly had any friends at school because the group I was hanging with was from my neighborhood, not the school. My mom barely spoke to me anymore, and neither did my younger sister.

I don't know, I just found myself one day cleaning out my room. The mess actually bothered me. When my girlfriend called, I started telling her I didn't feel like going out, because I really didn't. The more I hung around at home, the more my family talked to me. I started to talk with them—you know, just little stuff. When I answered them without snapping, they got more comfortable around me. When they asked me stuff, I started to realize they really wanted to know the answer. It got to be easier and easier to say no when my girlfriend called. Over a few months, I just pulled out of it.

I guess that's good. What sucks is that I've spent all the rest of the time since that trying to make up, catch up, be somebody. I'll get there, but man, what a long way around I went.

As you discover more about yourself during your teen years, you'll be trying new things and expanding your idea of what you can do. You have choices about the types of things to explore. As you test out who you are and what you can be, you may be tempted to drink, use drugs, become sexually active, or take other risks. These risky behaviors might make you feel more together or powerful than you really are and can result in dangerous consequences, like drinking and driving, riding in a car with a driver who's high, or having unprotected sex.

If you want to be a risk-taker, if you're seeking adrenaline rushes and thrills, you can do so without turning to drugs and alcohol. Instead, take up a new sport like downhill skiing, bike racing, or rock climbing, or join a school or community team. If athletics isn't your thing, run for class president, start a band, take an art class, try out for a role in the school play, join the debate team, or get involved in your community. It's your choice: You can do things that put you and your future at risk, or you can do things that help you to grow, reach, and stretch yourself in safe and healthy ways.

"Curiosity is natural, and everyone has to take some risks to not live a sheltered life, but right now it's important to know what risks are appropriate for your age."
Candace, 15

Self-Esteem Problems

During puberty, many girls struggle with self-esteem problems. You may have a war of wide-swinging emotions going on inside of you because of hormonal changes. Your friendships with girls as well as boys are shifting. You're on new ground in all of your relationships—with girls, boys, siblings, parents, and adults in general.

The things that used to make you feel happy and secure (family, home) now make you feel childish and annoyed. You push them away, but then feel lonely and insecure. You try out behaviors that you think make you appear mature and cool, but you know deep inside that they're really not okay. Again, you're on shaky ground because you haven't done these things before. Whew! What a tough time. Normal, but hard to figure out.

"I'd say alcohol and drugs can cause you to do things you don't want to do."
Margaret, 14

26

These changes make many girls and young women more vulnerable to using alcohol and other drugs. On the surface, using may seem like a way to calm your fears and to belong. But in reality, alcohol and drug use can make growing up even harder.

ILENE: I Was Messing Everything Up Because of a Friend Named Janice and Pot

I come from a really great family. When I was 15, I didn't drink or use other drugs and neither did anyone I knew. I made friends with a new girl in my school, Janice, and my family ended up taking her in because her home life was so crummy. My friends tried to make room for Janice in our group, but Janice just made fun of them because they didn't smoke cigarettes, or drink, or use drugs. Janice smoked a lot of pot. I felt torn between my friends and Janice.

Slowly, I ended up spending more time with Janice and hanging out with her friends. I started smoking pot, dropping acid, and drinking. I smoked cigarettes, too. My grades dropped right away. I skipped classes and started to smoke pot during the daytime. I was fighting with my whole family all the time.

My parents had me change schools, but I still got in trouble. They threatened to kick both Janice and me out of the house and told us to find jobs. Well, I found a job I liked, but I lied on the application about my drug use. My drug test came back positive, and I was fired three days after I started work. I got really depressed.

My parents set me up with a counselor who said I should get an evaluation for depression. She told me to be honest about my drug use, too. Something about just getting that referral helped me—I felt better because I knew I was going to get help, I guess.

Well, a bunch of things started happening for the better, and all at once. I got put on medication for depression, and my parents told Janice she'd have to live somewhere else. The tenseness at home let up right away. It hasn't been too long since I quit drinking and using, but I can see a difference: I'm getting along with my family again, for starters. But one thing that's left over is that my memory is shot, maybe from all the pot smoking. I hope my memory will come back over time.

You know, now I can't believe what I did. I was messing everything up because of a friend named Janice and pot. In a period of a few months, everything in my life went downhill. I have a new idea of what a friend is now. A friend is someone who won't let you self-destruct. Good friends don't pull you down.

When Use Becomes Abuse

Say you're at a point where you're using alcohol and other drugs every once in a while—at parties, with friends, sometimes even alone at home. You may be wondering if your drug use is very serious or not. How can you tell when you've stepped over that line from use into abuse, maybe even into addiction?

People who treat addicted young people agree that it's very difficult to tell when a teen is addicted. In fact, some people define *any* use as abuse. They say that *no* use is the best policy. Why? Because it's really hard to sort out what's just normal adolescent development, how drinking and drug use might be masking or indicating other problems, and what might be true addictive behavior.

What's more important for you to know is that there's a line you can step over. That line is drawn somewhere between pleasure and pain, between *wanting to* and *needing to,* between intending not to use or drink and doing it anyway. Somewhere along the line, you end up losing control of the drug. The drug takes charge of you. That may take the form of promises you make—but can't keep—about not using or drinking. Or pretending to yourself that you can quit anytime when you can't. Or finding yourself choosing friends and activities based on whether or not you can drink or use drugs.

Addiction to drugs and alcohol is a *process.* It may start out like this: You drink or use drugs for the high, out of boredom, because you're curious, to numb painful feelings, etc. But over time, you use for a different reason: *because you need to.* If you think you might be addicted to drugs or alcohol, see the Checklist of Trouble Signs on page 31 to figure out if you need help.

"I don't want bad habits. I want to be in control of my life . . . not have something else control me."
Valorie, 15

29

DEB: I Gave It All Up for Cocaine

I'm 18 now. When I was younger, I had it all—varsity cheerleader, good looks, cute boyfriend, popular friends, great parents, good grades. Yeah, I had it all. I started partying after football games, like everybody else, or so I thought. Someone brought beer and other booze each time. Someone else started bringing pot. The parties were regular things, and so was the drinking and pot smoking.

Older kids started coming to the parties, and they brought acid. Then someone brought cocaine. Some kids started snorting lines. I did, too, and I got very addicted very fast. Everything else in my life went downhill, also very fast. I stopped studying, cut class, and argued with my parents. I partied every weekend and would even find a party when I could during the week.

At report card time, my parents discovered I had dropped from an A student to failing in most subjects. They put two and two together. They had me assessed for chemical use. It didn't take a rocket scientist to figure out I had a problem with cocaine addiction. I was referred to a treatment program, which I completed not too long ago.

When I got out of treatment, I was too embarrassed to return to my original high school so I went to an alternative school. I still attend an aftercare group. I haven't changed my friends, and I'm really afraid of using again. Right now, I'm working up the courage to try to find new friends.

I guess I feel now like I gave up a fun high school experience for cocaine. I think about how I could have continued being a cheerleader, going to dances and games, maybe even becoming homecoming queen. I gave it all up for cocaine. I wish I could do it over, but I'm also glad my parents stepped in when they did, before I harmed myself or someone else more than I already had.

A Checklist of Trouble Signs

Check "yes" for any statements that apply to you or your friend, and "no" for the statements that don't apply.

1. Change in friends ☐ **yes** ☐ **no**
2. Poor grades; getting in trouble at school ☐ **yes** ☐ **no**
3. Not interested in activities that you used to like ☐ **yes** ☐ **no**
4. Looking rough and not caring about your appearance ☐ **yes** ☐ **no**
5. Slurred speech, glazed eyes ☐ **yes** ☐ **no**
6. Not going home or not going to school ☐ **yes** ☐ **no**
7. Lying, cheating, stealing, or frequently borrowing money ☐ **yes** ☐ **no**
8. Thinking about the next time you'll be able to drink or use ☐ **yes** ☐ **no**
9. Drinking or using other drugs to relax, relieve stress, or soothe feelings ☐ **yes** ☐ **no**
10. Drinking or using drugs alone ☐ **yes** ☐ **no**
11. A change in personality while drinking or using ☐ **yes** ☐ **no**
12. Blackouts (unable to remember what happened while you drank or used) ☐ **yes** ☐ **no**
13. Able to drink a large amount, gulping drinks, or drinking until drunk ☐ **yes** ☐ **no**
14. Hiding alcohol or drugs to avoid running out ☐ **yes** ☐ **no**
15. Driving while drunk or high ☐ **yes** ☐ **no**
16. Trying to stop, or making promises to stop, but unable to ☐ **yes** ☐ **no**
17. Getting drunk or high when you didn't mean to ☐ **yes** ☐ **no**
18. *Needing to* drink or use other drugs ☐ **yes** ☐ **no**
19. Change in family relationships ☐ **yes** ☐ **no**

If you checked "yes" for even just a few of these statements, you or your friend may already be in trouble with drinking or drug use. Find an adult you trust and can talk to (a parent, relative, teacher, school social worker, doctor, counselor, etc.).

ROSA: Once I Started Drinking, It Wasn't a Choice Anymore

I was 15 when I started drinking. Wine coolers, beer, the usual. I thought of that stuff as harmless, just like drinking soda. I mostly just drank at parties on weekends, no big deal. When I was 16, I fell in with a different crowd of kids and started drinking more often, but still mostly on weekends.

Then, I don't know, something happened. I started feeling really depressed. I just didn't have any energy to do anything—physically or emotionally. Things I used to care about didn't mean anything to me anymore. I wasn't on a team or in a sport, so when I went to a game or a meet, it was always to watch someone else play or win or whatever. When I went to school events, it was always to watch someone else act in a play, or sing in the choir, or show their latest attempt at video production. Whatever. I don't know . . . I just wasn't interested in anything. Other people included.

There was some point in that time when I pulled inward. No, I remember the exact time when that started happening—it was when I started to drink by myself. I would get a bottle of whatever I could lay my hands on, I didn't care what it was, and take it to my room in my backpack. Then I'd just wait for the day to be over, say goodnight to my parents, make all the going to bed sounds, flick off the light, and drink. I hated the taste of the liquor. I gagged on gin. Whisky and scotch burned on the way down. But I liked the hard stuff, because with beer it took too long to get to that "I don't care about anything" point.

I could drink a lot, too, before I felt sick to my stomach. I almost never threw up. Every night, I drank until I felt queasy or knew I was ready to pass out. But I always managed to hide the bottles and open the window for air so the room didn't stink. Things looked normal in the morning when my mom came in.

I started screwing up an almost straight-A average. What happened was I started to have blackouts. I couldn't remember what I had studied the night before, so I flunked quizzes and big tests. Well, that doesn't need to happen too often before it shows up in crappy grades and notes being sent home.

The next year is just a hazy blur for me. My grades dropped, I stopped seeing my friends, I lied all the time about everything in order to get booze and drink it. My parents didn't catch on for the longest time that I was drinking. I was really smart about hiding it. I stayed over at my girlfriend's whenever possible or waited until my parents were asleep and then drank at night. By morning I was hungover, but they didn't smell it on me.

I finally got so depressed I could hardly function. My grades were down the tube, I had exactly zero friends, I was involved in absolutely nothing, and my parents yelled but I just plain didn't care. Then they finally took me off to a counselor who figured out the depression first but also guessed at the drinking.

I've been working with that counselor for a long time now. Getting some help with the depression has helped me get a grip. At least I feel like someone else knows what's going on with me and maybe has some ideas about what I can do to feel better. I drank and used drugs to feel better. Now I have to find ways to do that without the drink or the drug. That scares me sometimes, so I just try not to think about it.

Many people have asked me how it could have happened so fast and to "such a young person." I don't know for sure, but when I watch now how my friends handle drugs and alcohol, or just choose not to do either, I know I'm different. Once I started drinking, it wasn't a choice anymore. What I mean is that I didn't *want* alcohol, I *needed* it. Then once I had it, I didn't need anything or anyone else. Does that make sense?

If you or someone you know is in trouble with drugs or alcohol, the most important thing you can do right now is get some help. Talk to an adult you trust, seek professional treatment, find a self-help group, or call the following number:

- 1-800-NCA-CALL, or 1-800-622-2255, will connect you to the National Council on Alcoholism and Drug Dependence (NCADD). When you hear the voice mail prompt, dial 1 for the number of a treatment/counseling service in your ZIP code. The call is free, but you'll need to use a Touch-Tone phone.

For a more complete list of other hotlines, plus Web sites, see pages 57–59.

2

Relationships and Risk Factors

Your relationships with other people play a big role in decisions about your life. Parents, friends, and boyfriends can all influence what you do and the choices you make. The stronger and healthier your relationships are, the less likely you'll be to turn to alcohol and drugs in times of need. Instead, you can rely on your friends and family for help.

But what happens if these important people in your life are using? Do you automatically have to do the same? Definitely not! This chapter discusses how the relationships in your life can be positive or negative. It also explores relationship "risk factors," or dangers, that may make you more likely to abuse alcohol and drugs.

"Always be yourself no matter what."
Keisha, 15

Staying Loyal to Girlfriends

Throughout your life, the relationships you have with other girls and women are important. Your bonds with them can help shape your views about the world and help you to understand your own thoughts and feelings. You need friends who are there for you, who will listen and give advice, and who know you well enough to be able to tell you when you're out of line or need help. Be loyal to your girlfriends. They offer a solid source of support and a sense of belonging that you can depend on.

When you're dating, it's sometimes tempting to put your friendships on hold. But when you do that, you send a message to your girlfriends that they're unimportant and can be set aside when something more interesting comes along. Each time you send that message, you make your friends feel insignificant and you damage your bonds with them.

Take some time to set your priorities straight when it comes to your relationships with both boys and girls. The stronger your friendship bonds are, the better position you'll be in to make good decisions when it comes to alcohol and drug use. And this takes finding friends you are loyal to, and who are loyal to you.

So what do you do if some of your friends are using? What if they want you to use, too? Just because they're drinking and doing drugs doesn't mean you automatically have to as well. You are your own person, and good friends should respect that. Tell your friends that you have the right to make choices about what you take into your body.

If one of your friends is seriously abusing drugs or alcohol, you might have to step in. Your friend may not know how to find help on her own, or even be aware that she needs it. There's a checklist on page 31 that can help you determine if a friend of yours is in trouble with drinking or drugs. You can fill out the checklist on your own, or with your friend. If you think your friend needs professional help, tell her your concerns and get the support of an adult you both trust.

If none of these solutions work, if your friend continues abusing drugs and alcohol, you may have to find another group to hang out with. To meet new people, get more involved at school and in your community. Join a sports team, explore theater or music, become a member of a club, find a job, or try out new activities.

CINDY: Tripping on Weekends in My Basement Became a Regular Thing

I'm 17. I never was a great student, and I never really liked school. My grades were always just average or below average, and I hung out with friends who would rather party and have a good time than study. It was great, so I thought. I was part of a group of eight or ten friends. We started using pot during seventh grade. By the time I had squeaked by to my sophomore year, we were bored with pot—though we still needed pot to get through the day. Pot made you feel mellow, like nothing could cause any feelings of fear or anxiety (except when and where you were going to smoke the next joint).

One night, we were hanging out in my basement. My parents were gone for the evening. A friend whipped out a sheet of paper with what looked like stickers on it. We each peeled one off, found a comfy spot, and proceeded to trip out on LSD. It was unreal. The walls seemed to breathe, and the clock seemed to melt into the wall. Colors were vibrant, so much more vivid than in real life. The guy next to me looked like a purple and black monster with big green teeth. I actually thought it was awesome.

Tripping on weekends in my basement became a regular thing. We all bragged about it, thinking we were so cool. One day in math class, I looked at the clock and had a flashback. The clock began melting into the wall just like it did on my first trip. It really freaked me out. I knew what a flashback was, but I didn't really believe it would happen to me. Then I noticed that when I saw bright colors, they would start moving like waves—more flashbacks.

I really began to freak when one weekend one of our friends went hyper on us. He was having a bad trip and just kept screaming and crying, and scream-ing and crying. After that weekend experience, and with my continuing flashbacks, I decided I didn't want to do LSD anymore. I was really afraid I would have a bad trip like my friend, and that I would keep having it in a flashback. So I went back to smoking pot, while the rest of the group continued to do acid.

That got boring for me real fast. It wasn't fun watching everyone else trip while I sat there. Slowly, I quit hanging out with them on weekends. It was a tough decision, but I didn't want to end up fried or dead. For a while, I spent a lot of time alone—my par-ents couldn't figure it out. Eventually, I started hang-ing out with other friends who might light up a joint once in a while, but not every weekend.

I've noticed that I feel better now and have more energy. It's easier to study, and my grades have come up (a bit). I guess it would be better to quit using altogether. I'll consider that.

Dealing with Boyfriends

At this time in your life, you're probably forming stronger relationships with guys. You may be dating casually or seeing someone seriously. If the guy you're involved with is drinking, using drugs, or smoking cigarettes, it can be extremely hard for you to avoid doing the same.

But you can take charge of what you put into your body. It's okay not to let anyone else tell you what to do or how to be. It's also okay not to participate in the same activities as your boyfriend. Allow your wants and needs to be a top priority in your relationship.

If a guy you're involved with gives you a hard time about your choices, drop him or ask him to change his behavior. If he can't give up drinking or drugs, maybe he needs help. Use the Checklist of Trouble Signs on page 31 to figure out if his problem is serious. On pages 57–59 is a list of hotlines and Web sites you can go to. Don't be afraid to ask an adult you trust to get involved.

"My friend Eddy talked me into trying heroin just once— said he'd shoot me up so I didn't have to do the needle part. I thought, 'Why not?' Big mistake. I got such a rush, and that's where trouble starts. You immediately want another hit to keep the feeling rolling."
Elena, 16

ANGELA: I Lived with This Guy for Six Months, and All We Did Was Smoke Pot

My mom and dad divorced when I was young. I lived with Mom, but she was an alcoholic and just couldn't function most days. I spent my early teens taking care of her. By the time I was 17, I just got sick of it.

I was dating a guy who was a couple years older, and he'd been bugging me to move in with him. One day, I finally decided, "Yeah, that's what I'm gonna do," and I did it that same afternoon. I had him meet me after school and drive me home. I knew Mom would be gone, so I sailed in there, threw a few things in a suitcase, and left.

I lived with this guy for six months, and all we did was smoke pot. We started to argue, then fight, and the next thing I knew we broke up and I moved back home. I've tried to sort all that out, and I realize that all we had in common was pot. I don't think it was possible for us to even have a relationship because we were high all the time. He was my using partner. Smoking pot ruined that relationship and made all of my other problems that much worse—not doing well in school, fights with my mom, and so on.

I decided I didn't want to end up like my mom. I quit using, and I haven't used since. I quit smoking, too. I want to get my life straightened out. I guess you could say the breakup helped me quit using. I realized there's more to a relationship than pot.

Unsafe Choices About Sex

"You have to be careful and learn to take responsibility for your actions."
Juana, 18

Alcohol and other drug use makes it hard to think clearly and to make good choices, especially when it comes to sex: Should I go to that party tonight? Should I check out whether a parent is going to be around? Should I drive my own car? Should I let that guy take me home? Should I have sex with this guy even though we just met?

When you're using, you're in greater danger of having unplanned sex. It could be easier for a guy to talk you into something you don't really want to do. You may tell yourself that it's worth the risk or that "It'll be okay this once." But unplanned sex often means that condoms aren't used, which can result in a sexually transmitted disease (STD) or pregnancy.

Not only are you more vulnerable to getting pregnant, but the fact that you were drinking or using other drugs at the time of conception or during your pregnancy may cause problems for your baby. Both Fetal Alcohol Syndrome (FAS) and Fetal Alcohol Effects (FAE) can permanently damage your child's development.

Marijuana can also harm your baby. Like alcohol, it easily crosses the placenta into the fetus. Marijuana also passes into breast milk. A baby exposed to the drug might be born smaller than average, cry and tremble more than other infants, and experience health and learning problems. Smoking pot regularly can also interfere with ovulation, affecting your periods.

Fast Facts

- 11 percent of babies born each year have been exposed to illegal drugs before birth.

- Children whose mothers used marijuana regularly during pregnancy may have problems developing memory and verbal skills.

Risk Factors

Some relationships can have a very negative impact on your life. For example, you may have a parent who's an alcoholic or who simply isn't around. Maybe your family has a history of violence and/or abuse. These problems, or risk factors, can make you more likely to use drugs and alcohol. This section describes four risk factors that involve girls and relationships, and what you can do if you need help.

"If you get too deep into drinking and using, it makes the problems you have now even worse."
Jackie, 16

41

1. Parents Who Use

Girls and young women who drink or use drugs often have parents who do. When the role model for drug and alcohol use is sitting right at home, you have some extra work to do to avoid following the same path.

"I want to be happily married with some little children. I want to study and gain knowledge, get a Ph.D., and become the right sort of me."
Titra, 14

First, take a look at the scene. Does the parent who drinks or uses other drugs have the kind of life you hope to have? Is he or she the kind of person you hope to be? Has he or she been the kind of parent and spouse you want to be someday? You have a choice about who you're going to become. If the role models in front of you are something less than what you want, learn from them. Don't do what they do. Study them. Figure out what they're doing that defeats them. And then do things differently.

It's a fact that if you have a parent with an alcohol or drug problem, you are genetically more likely to develop the same problem. The solution is to avoid drinking or using other drugs. If you know you're more vulnerable to becoming addicted than the average person, avoid using mood-altering chemicals of any kind.

If you're worried about a family member's drinking, contact Alateen, a support group for teenagers. To request information or find out where Alateen meetings are held in your area, call toll-free 1-800-344-2666. Alateen meetings can help you understand the situation better and will offer you support. You may call from either a Touch-Tone or rotary phone.

LEAH: I Was Hooked with That First Line

I started drinking at age 12. My parents are alcoholics (though I didn't know it then), and it was okay to drink around them. At our house, everyone, including my two older brothers, drank. I started smoking pot when I was 13, mostly with my brothers. I thought I was so cool because I had two brothers who were showing me the way, and my parents couldn't have cared less.

By the time I reached high school, my friends and I were drinking a bottle of wine and smoking a few joints before school to get us started. Then we would smoke a few more joints at lunch to get us through the day. It never stopped. We just kept lighting up more often to get us through whatever came next. Somehow, I managed to graduate from high school and get a job.

At a party one night just after I turned 18, a friend introduced me to cocaine. I loved it from the first line I ever snorted. I loved the feeling. It gave me so much nonstop energy. I was hooked with that first line. But of course I didn't realize it back then.

I started out snorting one to two lines a day. But the more I did, the more I wanted. With cocaine, I felt I could do anything. I felt like Superwoman. I did more and more, but eventually the high just wasn't there. I was building up a tolerance to the drug. After about a year and a half of snorting on a regular basis, I was up to 3 grams a day (20 to 30 lines). I had developed a very expensive habit.

I went weeks without sleeping, and I was sick all the time with colds and flu. My color was gray. I got bad nosebleeds and had to wait to snort another line (which was hell). They say you don't quit snorting until you hit rock bottom—by trying to kill yourself or kill someone else. That's what happened to me. I had stolen money for my habit and needed more. I felt nothing was worth living for and no one would understand what I was going through. I felt I wasn't good for anything, I was physically ill, and I didn't want to live.

One night, I wrote good-bye letters to all of the special people in my life—my family, friends, and boyfriend. I took a whole bottle of aspirin. That night,

I puked my guts out and ended up in the emergency room. From there I went directly into a treatment program. I was 19.

At first, I was in complete denial about my addiction. But, eventually, I started to feel really safe in treatment because I had no contact with the outside world. I worked with a counselor three times a day and after three weeks ended up in a group. The treatment program did the AA Twelve Step program, and I ended up talking through my life. By sharing it, I felt like a new person—a huge load had been lifted from my shoulders.

I wish I could say all of it was easy, but that would be a lie. I still have days when I crave a line because I loved the high of cocaine. Sometimes it's really hard because now I'm the "black sheep" of the family because I don't drink or use. In order to stay straight, I had to change my friends and that was incredibly difficult. I still get nosebleeds, and my mind isn't as sharp as it could have been—as it once was. My sense of smell isn't the same.

I know I've been given another chance at life, and I don't want to blow it by using again. In treatment, my counselor gave me a copy of a meditation book. I start each day by reading a page from this book. It helps me get through the day and makes life a bit easier.

2. Physical and Sexual Abuse

Girls who've been physically or sexually abused at some point in their lives are more likely to have social, emotional, and sexual problems. If you are being (or have been) abused by a family member or another trusted person, or if you've been through date rape or rape, get help right away. You can go to the police, a community health clinic, sexual violence center, a counselor or social worker, or a legal aid office. You can also look in the Yellow Pages under "Crisis Intervention Services" or "Child Abuse" for a number to call.

If you don't get help, you might get trapped in a cycle of abuse and victimization. During the healing process, you'll recognize that the abuse or rape wasn't your fault, learn what a healthy relationship is, and figure out how to cope with your painful feelings.

DEE: Alcohol Made Me a Prime Target

I started drinking when I was 14. For some reason, I just started drinking hard liquor right away—usually straight vodka. A friend of mine told me to come over to a house where she often went for drinking parties. I don't even know whose house it was, it was just some place where we could go and drink. I started going there all the time. There were always a lot of people at the house, most of them older.

We played a lot of drinking games at the parties. Most of the games ended up with everyone getting drunk. I started having blackouts where I'd wake up the next morning and couldn't remember anything about the night before.

Then one Saturday morning—a morning after I'd been drinking at this same house—I woke up and really hurt. I was bruised and felt lousy, but I had no memory of what happened the night before. My girlfriend called me and asked me if I was okay. I had to ask her why. She told me that a guy at the party had tried to rape me, and she and her boyfriend had broken it up and got me home. This guy waited until I got totally smashed during one of the drinking games and then made his move. I didn't remember a thing.

That did it for me. I quit drinking. I realized in that instant that I was being taken advantage of. Alcohol made me a prime target. I went through a lot more after that—depression and treatment for the drinking problem. One thing I know today is that drinking wasn't worth it. I ended up getting hurt.

3. Family Violence

Family violence is another risk factor for teen girls. If you've experienced violence in your family—either as a victim or as a witness—you're more likely to abuse alcohol and drugs. For help, look under "Crisis Intervention Services" in the Yellow Pages and find a number to call. Some phone books list a Crisis Intervention phone number inside the front cover.

4. Lack of Caring Adults

Girls who don't have a caring adult in their lives are also more likely to abuse alcohol and other drugs. Teen girls need at least one adult who cares about them and offers help during times of need. If you don't have a strong relationship with your parents, you may wonder who you can turn to when you need adult help. Even when it seems like there's no one in your life who cares, don't give up. Think of other adults you can reach out to: a relative, family friend, teacher, clergy member, counselor, school social worker, mentor, your doctor, or your principal.

Some risk factors are beyond your control—after all, you can't exactly *choose* your family. But you can choose the ways in which you cope with your problems. Even if you're dealing with difficult family issues, you don't have to end up using or abusing drugs. You have the power to make choices that will lead to a better future.

3

How to Say No to Alcohol and Other Drugs

No. Sometimes that tiny little word is so hard to say. You're at a party and someone calls you over and hands you a beer, or a joint, or something stronger. What do you say? Or you're at a friend's house and she's so excited for you to try something. That something turns out to be coke or speed. What do you do?

"Alcohol and drugs? They're nothing special." Allyson, 15

You're going to face situations like these at some point in your life. Making wise choices means deciding where you stand on alcohol and drug use ahead of time. Even then, it can be tough to say, "No, thanks. I don't want to." Saying it once is hard enough. When friends keep asking, and then the asking turns into people making fun of you, the "just say no" task gets even harder.

BRENDA: I Just Don't Want to Drink

I'm 15. No one in my family drinks or uses drugs of any kind. I don't drink or use because I think if I did, it would screw up my life, and I believe I have a lot going for me. I also hang out with a group of kids who don't drink, or smoke, or do drugs.

I started dating a guy two years older than me, a really nice guy with a screwed-up family and a history of using and trouble. Eric drank, smoked pot, and experimented with other drugs. He's been in treatment and kicked out of his house—but he's a really nice guy.

Well, my friends got concerned that I would turn into a druggie by hanging around with Eric, so they talked to me and got peer counselors and even the school social worker to talk to me. They just plain got on my back about dating Eric. Well, I chose not to use or drink, but I did go places with him where that was happening.

One night, Eric called me and asked me to go to a party with him, a kegger. I said, "No, I don't want to go." He said, "Why not? It'll be fun, come with me." I said no again. Well, he called a few more times, begging me to go with him to this party. I told him, "No, I don't want to go. You can come by, but you know I don't drink." He asked me, "Why? What's wrong with it?" I told him, "I just don't want to drink. I have some values I'm going to hold on to until I'm an adult." He asked, "Like what?" I said, "Like I don't plan on smoking, drinking, or using drugs. And I don't plan on having sex until I'm an adult."

Well, there was this looonnnng silence on the phone, and then Eric said, "Wow! I've never dated anyone like you before." We laughed about that. But I never did let him draw me into the using scene. I cared a lot about this guy, but I cared a lot about myself, too. I had to make a choice. I chose myself over this guy and drug use. We broke up eventually, but we talk and we're still friends.

Reality Check

Many girls feel pressured to use. But remember that *most girls don't drink or do drugs.* You may feel alone when you're at a party, a bunch of people are drinking, and the main topic of conversation seems to be who's doing what drug. When you hear the "Just one won't hurt" routine, or "Everybody's doing it," remember that it's up to you whether to buy into it. Following are some myths and reality checks about using.

"I've chosen not to depend on drugs."
Lena, 17

⊗ **Myth** You have to use drugs for a long time before they actually hurt you.

⊕ **Reality check** Some drugs can instantly cause your brain to send the wrong signals to your body. This can lead to a coma or a heart attack, and can make a person stop breathing.

⊗ **Myth** Drinking and drug use helps you fit in and make friends.

⊕ **Reality check** Learning good social skills helps you fit in and make friends.

"Drinking and using drugs may give you a high, but your high can be on life."
Pam, 15

49

⊗ **Myth** If you get drunk, a few cups of coffee can sober you up.

⊕ **Reality check** Once alcohol enters your blood-stream, time is the only thing that will help you to get sober.

⊗ **Myth** Sophisticated girls drink and do drugs.

⊕ **Reality check** Girls who lack confidence, are scared, and are covering for other problems are often the ones who use.

⊗ **Myth** As soon as you feel normal, the drugs you took are out of your body.

⊕ **Reality check** Drugs remain in your system long after the effects stop being felt. For example, cocaine can be found in your body up to one week after a single use.

⊗ **Myth** Alcohol is safer than other drugs.

⊕ **Reality check** Many teens who drink alcohol die in car accidents, commit suicide, or experience violent deaths.

⊗ **Myth** Pot isn't as bad for you as cigarettes are.

⊕ **Reality check** Marijuana smoke has more cancer-causing chemicals in it than tobacco smoke does.

⊗ **Myth** Teenagers are too young to get addicted to drugs and alcohol.

⊕ **Reality check** You can get addicted at any age. Even unborn babies can become addicted to a drug, if their mother is a user.

⊗ **Myth** Being able to drink more alcohol or use more drugs than anyone else at a party is cool.

⊕ **Reality check** Drinking or using more drugs indicates increased tolerance, a sign of addiction.

⊗ **Myth** You could try crack once, to see what it's like, and not get hurt.

⊕ **Reality check** Even one hit of crack can kill you. Crack can also be more addictive than heroin.

⊗ **Myth** Alcohol and drugs make sex more fun.

⊕ **Reality check** Alcohol and drug use more often impairs sexual functioning as well as the ability to make safe choices about sex.

⊗ **Myth** Using speed makes you feel alert and happy.

⊕ **Reality check** Speed can cause wild mood swings, halluci-nations, and nervousness.

⊗ **Myth** Wine coolers, beer, and pot are okay to use during pregnancy. It's the harder stuff that causes problems for the baby.

⊕ **Reality check** Wine coolers and beer contain the same drug that hard liquor contains—alcohol. Alcohol in any form and marijuana can harm an unborn baby.

Ten Tips for Saying No

You already know it's hard to say no. But you CAN do it. Refusing to use drugs and alcohol isn't something you need to feel ashamed about. In fact, you should feel great about it! You're showing that you intend to be somebody and to make something of your life. Following are ten tips for saying no.

1. Think Ahead

Any upcoming activity deserves some advance thought and planning. Where are you going? Who's going to be there? Are the parents home? Will alcohol or other drugs be available? Are you going with at least one good friend, someone you can rely on to back you up in saying no? How are you getting there and back? Is there a chance you'll have to catch a ride with someone who's drunk or high? Is there an adult you can trust and call if needed?

2. Have Alternate Plans

If you decide to attend a party or other event, have a back-up plan ready. Sometimes the best plan is to simply leave the party. You need to be prepared for this, though. Who can you call for a ride home if you need one? Do you have money for a pay phone and a taxi? What if your friend goes off and leaves you alone in a situation you don't like? Can you drive yourself or have a parent drive you so you're in control of your exit? Do you have an agreement with a trusted adult you can call?

3. Do Something Else

If you decide you shouldn't attend an activity, are you going to sit around feeling lonely and miserable? Make your own party. Call a few friends and do something you like. Don't sit around moping.

4. Get Involved

Sports, acting, singing, dance, gymnastics, writing—the list of possible activities is endless. So get involved. What you do isn't as important as how you feel while you're doing it. Find any activity you enjoy.

When you're active, you won't have time to fool around with drinking and drugs. Do things that give you a chance to show off a little; work at something and stick with it. If you feel good about some skill or talent, you won't reach for alcohol and other drugs to make you feel special, accepted, or popular.

5. Value Individuality

"If I could imagine myself in any way, it would be as a drug-free person who doesn't smoke. I think I would have such a better life."
Trish, 17

Many teens seek safety in looking, acting, and being just like everyone else. It takes a strong sense of self, a good sense of humor, and some self-confidence to stand up and do things differently. Go beyond experimenting with clothing and hair, and learn to think and act independently. It's a hard thing to do, especially when all you really want to do is fit in. But work on it. Ask yourself, "What do *I* think? What do *I* want? Is that what or how *I* want to be?" When you learn to think your own thoughts, it will be far easier to make good, self-caring decisions about using alcohol and drugs.

6. Decide What a Friend Is

What does having friends mean to you? Do you want friends so you can be part of a group? Do you want to be liked, in a general sort of way? If so, you'll be more likely to just do whatever the group is doing so you belong and have "friends." But friends are people who value you as much as you value them. True friendship means you care about each other and respect each other's thoughts and feelings. Make a pact with your friends not to drink and do drugs. Help each other keep the promise.

7. Practice Saying No and Don't Worry About Being Polite

Girls are often taught to please others and be polite. So saying no doesn't always come naturally—and saying no in a firm and not-so-polite way can be really uncomfortable. Give it some practice! Decide how to say no in various situations—decide exactly what words and phrases to use. Then practice them in a mirror, with your friends, or with your parents. Practice until the words roll off your tongue and feel natural. Start with these:

- "Thanks, but I already have something to drink."
- "I don't drink/I don't do drugs."
- "No way! Forget it."
- "Thanks, but I'll pass."
- "Thanks, but no thanks."

8. Help Someone Else

Be supportive of others. For example, if any of your friends are trying to give up alcohol and drugs, stand by them. Make a promise to watch out for each other during social situations where you might be tempted to use.

There are many other ways to be a supportive person. Volunteer to help a neighbor or donate time to help someone in need. Look around at home, at school, and in your neighborhood for opportunities to help others. The more involved you are in life, the less time you'll have for drugs and alcohol.

"If I had to give one piece of advice to my younger sister about drinking or using drugs, I'd tell her this: 'Just don't get started!'"
Courtney, 13

9. Face Your Problems and Your Feelings

Alcohol and other drug use is often just a sign that something else is wrong. If you find yourself drinking or using because it makes you feel better or because it pushes problems away, then get real help—from another person, not a substance.

Remember that alcohol is a depressant. If you're drinking to relieve sadness or stress, alcohol can leave you feeling worse than ever. The same is true for other drug use. The drugs may give you a brief high, but it always ends. And when it does, you face the same issues you were trying to escape. Using these substances often leads you into other trouble that can make your problems more difficult to solve.

10. Realize You're Not Alone

Sometimes you might feel like the only one who isn't using. Make an effort to get to know other girls and young women who want to stay away from drugs and alcohol. Or, reach out to an adult you're close to and share your feelings with that person. Don't be afraid to get the support you need.

How to Get Help

If you think you need help with drinking or drug use, or if you have a friend who needs help, talk with an adult you trust. Using can be a sign of other, deeper problems. A parent, teacher, doctor, school counselor, student assistance coordinator, school nurse, school social worker, clergy member, or therapist can help you sort things out.

The adult you talk to might recommend that you go into treatment for a drug or alcohol problem. This would probably involve going to a hospital or clinic, where you would talk to a counselor or get involved in group therapy. During treatment, you'll learn about drug and alcohol abuse, talk about your problems, and work toward solutions.

If these options aren't possible for you at this time, you can turn to a national hotline or information line for help. Also listed in this section are World Wide Web sites you can explore, if you have access to a computer and the Internet.

Hotlines

In addition to the numbers below, you can look in your phone book for toll-free drug information hotlines. Check your Yellow Pages under "Drugs" and "Alcohol" for local helping resources, too. Remember that 800 numbers are toll-free, so there's no charge for the call and it won't show up on your phone bill.

- 1-800-COCAINE, or 1-800-262-2463, will connect you with a counselor who can give you guidance and refer you to a local treatment center. This hotline is operated by Phoenix House, one of the largest private, nonprofit drug abuse service agencies in the U.S. The phones are staffed 24 hours a day. On the World Wide Web go to: *http://www.riverhope.org/phoenix/*

- 1-800-662-HELP, or 1-800-662-4357, is the number for the Center for Substance Abuse Treatment (CSAT) of the Substance Abuse and Mental Health Services Administration. You will hear a recording that leads to more options, including alcohol/drug information, treatment options in your state, and telephone counseling. Call from a Touch-Tone phone.

- 1-800-347-8998 connects you to Cocaine Anonymous. Their answering service will refer you to a Cocaine Anonymous office in your area, so you can find out where a group meets near you. On the World Wide Web go to: *http://www.ca.org/*

Info Lines

Below is a list of national organizations that offer information on alcohol, drugs, and substance abuse.

- 1-800-729-6686 connects you to the National Clearinghouse for Alcohol and Drug Information (NCADI), an organization of the federal government providing free information on substance abuse. Telephone information is available in both English and Spanish. This info line is open Monday through Friday 8 A.M. to 7 P.M. EST (except on government holidays). You may call from a Touch-Tone or rotary phone. On the World Wide Web go to: *http://www.health.org/links/reglink.htm*

- 1-800-788-2800 will connect you to all federal alcohol and drug clearinghouses (organizations that offer information on all aspects of alcohol and drugs). You will hear a recording with options for reaching various info lines and help lines. Call from a Touch-Tone phone.

Web Sites

Web sites are a great source of information and support. You'll need access to a computer and the Internet to explore these sites.

- Web of Addictions
  http://www.well.com/user/woa/
  Sponsored by Andrew L. Homer, Ph.D., and Dick Dillon, this award-winning site has loads of factual information on alcohol and drug abuse, including descriptions of drugs and their effects, in-depth information on special topics, links to other resources, and places to get help.

- Mental Health Net
  http://www.cmhc.com/selfhelp.htm

  Sponsored by CMHC Systems in Dublin, Ohio, this very helpful and user-friendly site has tons of links to sites with self-help information on a wide variety of health issues, including substance abuse. Links are organized by subject area, and rated on a four-star system based on quality of content and presentation.

- Nonprofit Resources Catalogue
  http://www.clark.net/pub/pwalker/Health_and_Human_ Services/Substance_Abuse/

  A good list of links to sites that offer substance abuse information, resources, personal stories, support groups, and recovery programs. Sponsored by Phillip A. Walker.

- Online AA Resources
  http://www.recovery.org/aa/homepage.html

  Sponsored by Online Recovery Resources, this site is a comprehensive collection of information on Alcoholics Anonymous (AA), including its philosophy, history, links to AA related resources, and how to find a chapter in your area.

- Al-Anon and Alateen
  http://solar.rtd.utk.edu/~Al-Anon/

  This site offers information on Al-Anon, a worldwide organization to support families and friends of alcoholics (whether or not the alcoholic is seeking help or even acknowledges that there's a problem), and Alateen (for younger members), including their philosophy, how to decide if the group is for you, and how to find a group in your area. Information on this site is available in six different languages.

"Smoking is a disgusting habit. It smells gross and tastes gross and looks stupid.

If you're trying to be a rebel, do something else."

Leslie, 15

Part Two

What You Should Know About **Smoking**

4

Hooked on Cigarettes— What It's Like

You've seen the billboards and magazine ads with beautiful, healthy looking models who are smoking. You've also seen girls smoking at school, at the mall, during rock concerts, in restaurants, and on the street. More than ever, girls are smoking, due in part to advertising campaigns that encourage them to. Today, the tobacco industry makes over $270 billion in profits each year from tobacco products sold to kids and teens.

But in fact, *most girls don't smoke.* So, even when it may look like everyone around you is smoking, most girls are choosing not to get hooked on cigarettes. This chapter talks about why girls smoke, the effects of smoking, and why it's important to quit (or not get started in the first place).

CHRISTY: I Felt Really Mature When I Smoked

Did I care that smoking was bad for me? No way! I was working as a waitress in my first job. I felt mature having a job, getting a paycheck, handling my own schedule. Well, all the older women I worked with smoked like fiends. The air in the break room was practically blue with smoke all the time.

It didn't take me long to try my first cigarette, then buy a pack. I smoked all the time at work, and my mom didn't know the difference because all my waitress clothes stunk like cigarettes whenever I came home from work anyway.

I felt really mature when I smoked. I liked the way the cigarette looked in my hand. And I liked the routine of twisting the top off a Coke, sliding an ashtray over to my side of the break table, and lighting up. I liked how I thought I looked. The fact was, I was mousy and didn't look especially tough or mature, so smoking made me at least think I looked older.

Anyway, I always thought I'd just quit whenever I wanted to. Only I never wanted to. Then I got interested in the swim team at school. Well, they've got rules, you know—the first one being no alcohol or drugs, the second one, no smoking. I really wanted to join the team, so I told myself, "Oh, okay, I'll just quit smoking then." So I signed up and then started playing games with quitting: I'll just finish this pack and then I'll quit tomorrow. I won't smoke before swim practices, just after. I'll cut down. And on and on.

I had to hide my smoking so no one on the team or the coach found out. I felt stupid going to such lengths to hide it, but I couldn't quit just like that. I'd get really crabby and on edge whenever I'd go for a couple hours without a smoke. I also couldn't breathe, and I had a hard time keeping up. I was hooked, and I was getting kind of desperate to quit. Kids who think they can quit any time are kidding themselves.

My girlfriend (who's a great swimmer) finally helped me quit. I could have killed her at the time, but she told the coach I was trying to quit and having trouble. He pulled me aside, figured out right away that I was serious about wanting to quit, and helped me do it. He gave me a booklet that showed how to go about quitting and what to expect. Then he set goals for me and had me check in.

That extra help was what I needed to quit, but it really was hard—hard enough for me to be sure I never want to start again because I never want to have to stop again.

Why Some Girls Smoke

The 1995–96 PRIDE Survey found that over 29 percent of junior high girls were smoking cigarettes and that more than 47 percent of senior high girls were smoking. Of the over 60,000 girls questioned, more than 22 percent said they smoked every day. According to the survey, when it comes to the number of teens who are smoking, girls have caught up with boys.

Many young women start smoking because it makes them feel more mature, tough, and cool than they really feel inside. But teens who smoke cigarettes have smoke breath, their clothes and hair smell like cigarettes, and their fingertips can turn yellow from nicotine stains. (*Not* cool.) And studies have shown that many teens who smoke:

- use other drugs,
- have risky sex,
- get into fights,
- carry weapons,
- do poorly in school,
- have a poor self-image, and
- lack confidence.

Here are the five major reasons why teens smoke:

1. because their friends, peers, or family members do,
2. because they want to see what it's like,

3. because they think it's cool,

4. because it's easy for them to get cigarettes, and

5. because tobacco ads glamorize smoking.

Cigarette ads are very deceiving, so don't let yourself be fooled. These advertisements often show attractive, well-dressed people who look successful, athletic, sexy, and healthy. But is being hooked on tobacco really a sign of success? How many athletes do you know who smoke? Is a cigarette hanging out of someone's mouth sexy? How can a habit that kills *over 1,000 people* every day be healthy? The ads, while not exactly truthful, are designed to do one thing: sell cigarettes.

Many people across the U.S. are angry that tobacco companies glamorize smoking. For example, six years after Virginia Slims cigarettes were introduced as a cigarette for women, twice the number of teenage girls were smoking. And recent studies reported in the *Journal of the American Medical Association* have shown that the cartoon character of "Joe Camel" has helped the R. J. Reynolds tobacco company sell Camel cigarettes to minors. (In fact, kids as young as three years old easily recognize Joe Camel.) People involved in antismoking campaigns hope these studies will prove that tobacco companies are aiming their ads at young people and should therefore be strictly regulated. Legislation is being introduced to give the Food and Drug Administration (FDA) the authority to set guidelines about how tobacco products are promoted.

Smoking is a habit that costs a lot of money, too. Today, a pack of cigarettes can cost between two and three dollars.* More than 26 billion packs are sold every year in the U.S. You do the math. No wonder

"I quit smoking because I figured big tobacco companies don't deserve my money."
Diane, 16

---

*These prices are as of 1997. Prices are going up as states continue to levy higher taxes on cigarettes.

tobacco companies have so much money to spend on advertising!

The more you smoke, the more cigarettes you have to buy. Your healthcare costs go up, too. If you smoke, you'll have more respiratory problems, so you'll probably spend more money on cough drops, cold medicines, allergy treatments, and visits to the doctor.

Fast Facts

The average smoker spends $500 to $700 per year on cigarettes. With $500, you could:

- enjoy 83 movies,
- rent 125 videos,
- buy a racing bike or a canoe,
- attend 12 concerts, or
- buy a plane ticket and a suitcase.

"Smoking is too expensive."
Whitney, 16

What's the Big Deal?

"Smoking causes cancer and ashtray breath."
Liz, 16

You may feel like tuning out when someone tells you about what happens to you when you smoke. You might decide not to listen because: A) you think none of the bad things will happen to you, B) you intend to quit when you're older, so it's no big deal if you smoke now, or C) the health problems caused by cigarettes affect adults, not teens.

In fact, the U.S. Surgeon General has studied young people who smoke. These are some of the problems that can and do happen to teens who smoke:

- decreased physical fitness,
- increased coughing and phlegm,
- increased respiratory problems such as colds, bronchitis, and pneumonia,

- development of artery disease, which often leads to heart disease, and

- slow lung growth, which prevents lungs from functioning normally.

Years of smoking can cause cancer and heart disease, and can lead to an early death.

Even with your very first drag on a cigarette, you'll be likely to experience coughing, dizziness, shortness of breath, and nausea. Don't forget the other gross aspects of smoking: bad breath, clothes that smell of

"I don't
want to die
young, so
I don't
smoke."
Briana, 17

tobacco, coughing, phlegm in your throat, hair that stinks, and burn holes in your clothes. And the people around you who don't smoke will probably think you're gross for polluting the air.

What many teens (not to mention adults!) don't realize is that nicotine—the substance found in all forms of tobacco (including smokeless tobacco, or "chew")—is a drug that you can get hooked on like any other drug. But unlike other drugs, nicotine is widely advertised and promoted. This can make cigarettes seem less dangerous. The fact is tobacco smoke contains over 4,000 chemicals, including poisons like cyanide, formaldehyde, arsenic, and butane, as well as carcinogens (substances that cause cancer).

Smoking at an early age may lead to early use of other drugs. According to the Surgeon General's *Report for Kids About Smoking,* young people who smoke are:

- 3 times more likely to use alcohol,
- 8 times more likely to smoke pot, and
- 22 times more likely to use cocaine.

Maybe you're thinking that smoking every once in a while won't hurt, as long as you're careful and don't get carried away. But because nicotine is as physically addictive as heroin or cocaine, "once in a while" often becomes a lifetime habit. And psychologically, you quickly get used to the repetitive motions of smoking. Before you know it, you might end up smoking a pack a day (75,000 drags a year!). The sheer repetition of the habit makes it hard to break.

"I'll Quit When I'm Older . . . "

"I'll just quit when I'm older." The fact is that the earlier you start smoking, the more likely you'll be to continue smoking. The Centers for Disease Control predict that if you start smoking daily in high school, you'll keep smoking for at least another seven to nine years.

PROBLEM, I DON'T HAVE A PROBLEM. WHAT D'YA MEAN?

"I started smoking at 16 and thought it was okay. Then I got hooked. I couldn't wait for my next drag."
Britt, 17

JENNIFER: I Just Didn't Think of Cigarettes as a Drug

At 15, I started smoking—just like that. I went to a park every day after school with two of my friends. Angel whipped out a pack one day and passed it around. I didn't think anything of it at all. I just took the smoke and lit up. It tasted awful. When I think back now, I clearly remember hating it and feeling

69

that awful burning sensation in my lungs. I also remember wanting to cough and willing myself not to, so my friends wouldn't laugh at me.

You're going to laugh now, but I'm going to say it: I actually got my own pack and practiced smoking so I could do it without looking stupid. I didn't even know how to get that first pack, either. I was too embarrassed to try just buying a pack at the gas station. So I scoped out cigarette machines that were out of the way. In the end, I saw a pack on the dashboard of a car in a parking lot. I glanced around, and not seeing anyone, I reached in through the open side window and grabbed it.

After practicing, I could light up, inhale, and exhale like I'd done it forever, and I was ready to smoke in public. Not once did I think maybe I shouldn't be doing this. I just didn't think of cigarettes as a drug I could get hooked on.

Of course, I'd heard all the facts about cancer and all of that, but I didn't relate any of that to myself. Until I tried to quit, that is. I couldn't stop. The more I tried to quit, the more I failed. I finally got real serious about it and set some goals. The first two weeks of quitting, I was miserable. But I made it through. I can't for sure say that I'll never smoke again, even though I want to. It's just too hard to stop. But I'm hanging in there.

Here are three things you should know about starting to smoke early:

1. you'll have a harder time quitting,
2. you'll probably become a heavy smoker, and
3. you're more likely to get sick with a problem related to smoking.

Does everyone who smokes become addicted? Many do. Millions of people today are addicted to smoking. Those who want to quit have a really hard time doing so. According to the U.S. Surgeon General, half of all young people who smoke cigarettes say they want to quit but can't.

If you smoke—especially if you smoke every day—there's a good chance that you're addicted to nicotine. To know whether you're hooked, try quitting cold turkey. If you're addicted, you'll probably experience withdrawal symptoms (feeling tired, unable to concentrate, quick to anger, grouchy, depressed, and like you need another smoke). The good news is these symptoms won't last forever.

Fast Facts

- Smoking tobacco is the leading cause of preventable death in the U.S. Smoking causes more people to die each year than deaths from gunshot wounds, AIDS, and car and airplane accidents *combined*.

- From 1990–1993, more Americans died from smoking-related illnesses than were killed in all of the major U.S. wars in the history of our nation.

- Four out of every five people who use tobacco started before age 18.

- Most smokers (83 percent) wish they had never started smoking.

- 93 percent who try to quit start smoking again within one year.

- Of those who successfully quit smoking for one year or longer, two-thirds remain smoke-free.

The Three Great Myths About Smoking

Despite the constant warnings, many girls decide that there are positive aspects of smoking that outweigh the negative ones. They believe the "Three Great Myths About Smoking."

Myth #1: Smoking Relieves Stress

Reality: Smoking is simply something to do. It occupies your hands and involves a repetitive routine. The routine can seem soothing, but soon you're locked into a bad habit. The habit becomes a limitation: You can't end a meal, be at a party, or hang out with your friends unless you have a cigarette in your hand. Your dependency actually creates *more* stress in your life, as you try to figure out when and where you can light up your next smoke.

Myth #2: Smoking Helps You Lose Weight

Reality: Weight gain and weight loss have more to do with eating patterns than with smoking. Some people who smoke gain weight, and some lose it. And some people who quit smoking gain weight, but some lose it.

Smoking reinforces the need for oral gratification (keeping your mouth busy). So smoking can make it harder than ever to stop continual eating or snacking. And when you smoke, you don't feel much like exercising. Lack of physical movement can make you gain weight.

Myth #3: Smoking Helps You Belong

Reality: If you smoke just because your friends do, you're not thinking for yourself. Do your friends respect your individuality? If belonging to a group depends on whether you smoke, perhaps the ties that bind you to the group aren't very strong. Look around to find friends who don't smoke.

If you smoke because you think people will look up to you, you're making a decision based on impressing others, rather than on what you really want to do. (You're probably not impressing anyone anyway.) Instead, work on just being yourself.

The Truth About Secondhand Smoke

"Most kids don't realize how smoking affects their performance, especially in athletics."

Barbara, 17

Secondhand smoke is the smoke you're exhaling into a room—smoke that other people have to breathe. For many years, no one thought much about secondhand smoke. But recent studies have shown that breathing in the smoke from someone else's cigarette, cigar, or pipe can cause serious health problems, including lung cancer, heart disease, and respiratory infections. In fact, smoke-filled rooms can have as much as six times the air pollution of a busy highway.

Babies are also affected by "secondhand" smoke. Smoking during pregnancy can harm the fetus and lower a baby's birth weight. As many as 10 percent of infant deaths are now thought to be caused by the mother's tobacco use during pregnancy.

Fast Facts

- The Environmental Protection Agency (EPA) classifies secondhand smoke as a carcinogen. As a result, the EPA has recommended that smoking in public buildings be banned.

- The EPA has urged parents of young children not to smoke at home (or allow other adults to do so), because secondhand smoke causes an estimated 150,000 to 300,000 cases of pneumonia and bronchitis every year in children under 18 months old.

- Smoking around young children can slow their lung development.

The truth is that when you smoke, you hurt more than yourself. You pollute the air and risk the health of anyone who's around you when you smoke. The next chapter, "Staying Clean of Nicotine," offers tips for getting cigarettes out of your life.

5

Staying Clean of Nicotine

Staying away from cigarettes isn't easy, whether you've never smoked or you're a smoker who's trying to quit. For example, it's likely that if you're a nonsmoker, someone, somewhere will try to convince you to smoke one little cigarette, just for fun. Or, if you're already a smoker, someone, somewhere has probably told you to try to quit. Either way, it can be hard not to start and even harder to stop.

The best way to stay clean of nicotine is to learn all you can about its effects (see the previous chapter, pages 62–74, for more information). Also, be aware of what's causing you to smoke: Are you feeling stressed out? Trying to avoid your problems? Going along with the crowd? Attempting to feel more mature or in control of your life? If any of these reasons are influencing your actions, smoking isn't a solution.

Whether you're trying to avoid cigarettes or trying to quit smoking, seek the help of a friend. Having a supportive person by your side can help you to say no when a cigarette is offered or when you're craving nicotine. You can also be a friend or source of support for someone else. If you have a friend who's smoking too much, encourage her to give up cigarettes. Let her know that you'll stand by her every step of the way while she tries to quit.

"I've tried cigarettes, but I knew smoking would ruin my voice. I want to be a singer when I get older, so I stopped smoking."
Allie, 17

NICOLE: I Said, "I'll Be Your Quitting Buddy"

I'm 16, and I've never smoked. Why? My dad smokes, and I hate it. One of my best friends, Katy, started smoking when we were 14. She always made fun of me for not smoking. But I just didn't start. We both played softball and basketball, but Katy continued to smoke.

Then I listened to a drug prevention talk at my school, and for some reason I tuned in when the presenter started lecturing us about how we can help our friends by not drinking and using. I raised my hand (Katy was sitting in the desk right next to me) and asked, "But how can you help a friend who smokes and doesn't want to quit?" Katy turned beet red.

The presenter went to the blackboard and started outlining all the things the people in the group suggested. When we were done, we had outlined about ten things we could do to help. When they let us out, Katy was storming down the hall ahead of me. I caught up, and before she could yell at me I said, "Let's try it." "Try what?" she asked. I said, "I'll be your quitting buddy. You can call me every time you feel like lighting up."

Katy listed every reason she could think of for why quitting wouldn't work. What I thought was interesting, though, is that she never once said she didn't want to quit. She said other things like, "What if I want to smoke in the middle of the night . . . I can't call you then," and "I'm too used to it to stop now," and "I don't need to worry about it until I'm older," or "It relaxes me, so I'll be stressed if I stop."

I just waited her out and asked her when we should start. Then I suggested we start right then. She panicked and refused. So after school at the park, I took out a piece of paper and we worked out a two-week plan, so she had a chance to get used to the idea and to cut down. She reported in to me every day during our after-school park time. It was hard for her to quit because her parents both smoked at home. She screwed up twice by smoking more than she was supposed to, but we just got back to it.

On her quit day, I made her a card the size of a cigarette pack and told her to keep it where she usually kept her pack of cigarettes. On it I had written my phone number and a little poem for her, reminding her to keep at it. She called me a few times on weekends when it was especially hard, but mostly she just struggled through it.

At one point she really wanted to give up, so I told her we were going to start running. I set up a schedule, and we ran every day after school. I met her on Saturdays to run, too. The running helped her focus on something other than cigarettes. I almost lost my best friend, but we both stuck it out. Whoever thought quitting was easy is crazy.

Eight Tips for Avoiding Smoking

If you haven't started smoking, pay attention to everything you hear about not starting. When your school brings in speakers or finds other ways to give you information about nicotine and tobacco, listen! Learn as much as you can, keeping in mind that you have a choice to make.

To avoid smoking, you'll need to plan ahead. Someone might offer you a cigarette or ask you to try smoking "just once," so you'll have to be ready to resist. Following are eight tips for saying no.

1. Resist Curiosity

It's natural to want to try smoking once—you're probably curious about what it's like. People may tell you that it feels great, it's soothing, it's refreshing, or it's a rush. Here's what it's really like when you take your first drag: Your throat burns, your lungs feel like they're on fire, you cough, you feel sick, your eyes water, your heartbeat speeds up, and you become short of breath. And here's what it feels like to be a regular smoker: You cough every morning when you wake up (and throughout the day), you have nicotine cravings, you constantly need to find a time and place to smoke, and you experience wheezing and shortness of breath.

2. Hang Around with Nonsmokers

It's a lot easier to resist cigarettes when the people you hang out with don't have them. If most of your friends smoke, ask them to consider quitting and offer to help them.

But what happens if your parents smoke at home? You have a choice not to follow their example. Just because they smoke, just because it might be easy for you to get away with smoking at home, you can still choose not to start.

3. Find a Friend Who Will Support Your Decision Not to Smoke

When you have a supportive friend who can help you say no to cigarettes, it's much easier for both of you to resist smoking. Make a pact with your friend not to smoke. If you stick together, it will be harder for other people to tempt you to smoke.

4. Avoid Situations That Involve Smoking

Think twice before you go to a party or event where you know people will be smoking. Or, if your plans include hanging out with a group in which almost everyone smokes, change your plans. If a guy who's a smoker asks you out, think about whether you really want to date him. It's easy to pick up the cigarette habit when you spend a lot of time with someone who's always smoking around you.

5. Be Ready to Say No

When you say no firmly, instead of mumbling something like, "Well, um, I don't really know if I should," people will be more likely to respect what you're saying. Think up the words you'll use and practice saying no. A simple "No, thanks, I don't smoke" should work just fine.

6. Don't Believe the Media Hype

Look at the billboards and magazine ads that are selling cigarettes. Are those smiling, healthy faces with shining white teeth really true to life? (Do your teeth ever look white when you're staining them yellow by inhaling smoke?) A Marlboro Man died of lung cancer. Think of him each time you see a cigarette ad.

7. Stay Busy

When you're active, you don't have time to think about smoking. Join a sports team or exercise at home, get involved in after-school activities, or find hobbies you enjoy. If you're at a party where a lot of people are smoking, keep your hands and mouth busy. Talk, keep a soft drink in your hand, chew gum, etc.

8. Be Proud to Be a Nonsmoker

Don't feel guilty or insecure about your choice not to smoke. Instead, be confident that you've chosen to avoid a habit that's difficult to break and that negatively affects your health. Support others who choose not to smoke.

"If my younger sister told me she wanted to smoke, I'd tell her, 'It'll be the worst mistake you'll ever make. Don't do it.'"
Maria, 16

Six Tips for Quitting

If you're ready to quit smoking, you may want to join a stop-smoking program. But if paying for such a program or finding transportation isn't possible, you can try quitting on your own. Quitting smoking isn't easy under any circumstances, so find a supportive friend who can help you through the process. Here are six tips to get you going.

1. Choose a Day to Quit

"I always say I'll quit tomorrow or after I finish this pack, but it's so hard to quit."
Hannah, 15

By choosing a specific starting date, you'll be less likely to procrastinate. Choose whatever works for you: next Monday, your birthday, "Great American Smokeout" day (November 21), etc. Don't put it off.

2. Learn About Withdrawal Symptoms

Prepare yourself to quit by knowing what to expect. Withdrawal symptoms are a normal part of the quitting process, but they don't affect everyone in the same way. You may find yourself becoming irritable, craving cigarettes, feeling moody, etc. Some people even get headaches or want to snack continually. Remind yourself that these symptoms won't last long.

3. Take It Step by Step

You don't have to quit cold turkey, unless you want to. You can start by cutting your cigarette use in half the first week. Then continue to cut your use by one-half each week, until you're down to zero.

4. Keep Busy

Have plenty of activities lined up to help you through the first few days or weeks. Sports, exercise, or any physical activity can help. Plan your days carefully so your time is full. The busier and more active you are, the less time you'll have to think about cigarettes.

5. Get Support

You don't have to go through this alone! Tell your friends and family in advance that you're quitting, and ask them for their support. Have someone to call, talk to, and spend your free time with.

6. Avoid the Temptation to Smoke

Stay away from situations, people, events, and places that might tempt you to smoke. Ask your friends not to smoke in front of you.

Four Tips for Helping a Friend to Quit

Friends can have a tremendous influence when helping someone to quit smoking. So you have a role to play if you want to help a friend quit. Following are four ideas about what you can do.

"Smoking makes your breath stink and guys don't want to kiss you."
Grace, 16

1. Offer Support

Be there for your friend, but remember you can't *make* her quit. When she chooses to stop smoking, help her, but don't turn away if she starts smoking again. Most smokers have to quit several times before they can quit for good.

2. Check In

Let your friend know you're thinking about her. Send her encouraging notes, call her, and spend time with her as often as you can. Tell her you know that what she's doing is hard.

3. Be Encouraging

Praise your friend's efforts, assure her you know she can do it, and let her know you're pleased she decided to quit.

4. Help Her to Stay Active

Many people who quit smoking need other activities to fill up their time. In addition, many people who quit worry that they'll gain weight. Offer to jog with your friend or join a sports team with her. Suggest activities, especially physical ones, that get her out and moving. Show your support by joining her.

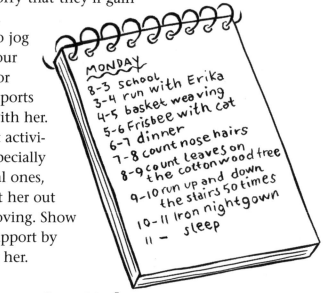

MONDAY
8-3 school
3-4 run with Erika
4-5 basket weaving
5-6 Frisbee with cat
6-7 dinner
7-8 count nose hairs
8-9 count leaves on
the cottonwood tree
9-10 run up and down
the stairs 50 times
10-11 Iron nightgown
11 — sleep

How to Get Help

Whether you're trying to quit on your own, or helping a friend who's ready to stop smoking, there are places you can go for help and information. Your family doctor can tell you about stop-smoking programs. Or you can look in your telephone book for organizations that offer information about such programs: Contact your local branch of the American Cancer Society, American Lung Association, and/or the American Heart Association.

You can also explore the World Wide Web, which offers many sites about smoking, tobacco and nicotine, tobacco advertising, and quitting. On the next page is a list of helpful Web sites to check out. You'll need access to a computer and the Internet.

"Make a smart decision not to smoke— smoking's just not worth it."
Andrea, 17

Web Sites

- The QuitNet
  http://www.quitnet.org
  Sponsored by the Tobacco Control Program at the Massachusetts Department of Public Health, QuitNet was developed to help people who want to quit smoking. They offer lots of interesting facts, helpful tips, resources, interactive tools, up-to-date news reports on related issues, a chat room for people who have quit or want to quit smoking, and more.

- Kickbutt
  http://www.kickbutt.org
  This site is sponsored by Washington DOC (Doctors Ought to Care) and was created to give young people accurate information about the physical and social effects of smoking, the tobacco industry's efforts to attract children and teens through advertising, how to quit smoking, how to get involved in anti-tobacco activism, links to other sites, and much more.

- The BADvertising Institute
  http://world.std.com/~batteryb/
  The BADvertising Institute was started by women who were disgusted by tobacco companies' efforts to market cigarettes and chewing tobacco to children and teens. The powerful images at this site will definitely make you think twice about the advertising you see— and give you motivation to quit smoking, or never start.

- NicNet Nicotine and Tobacco Network
  http://www.ahsc.arizona.edu/nicnet/
  This site, sponsored by the University of Arizona, offers information about the effects of tobacco use, a library of interesting news items and research related to tobacco, tips to help you quit, places to get help, and links to other good sites.

"Do you know who really looks like Barbie?

No one.

No one can have that body shape."

Angela, 17

Part Three

What You Should Know About Eating Disorders

6

Fixated on Food— What It's Like

"If you don't get messed up with eating problems, you can stay healthy and feel good."
Brit, 15

Through the years, adults have probably told you a lot about food: what to eat *(Eat your peas— they're good for you)*, how to eat it *(Use your fork, dear)*, when to eat *(Now—while it's hot or fresh or ripe)*, and how much *(Clean your plate)*. After constantly hearing about the importance of food, you might be asking yourself how food can possibly be a problem. But for many girls and young women, eating becomes a daily battle. Each day, these girls struggle with overeating, dieting, bingeing and purging, or starving themselves.

Even if you don't have problems with food yourself, you probably know at least one girl who does. The good news about eating disorders is that knowledge is power. The more you know about what eating disorders are and how someone acts when she's having a problem with eating, the more likely you'll be to prevent this from happening in your life. Your knowledge can also lead you to get help for a friend who's struggling with eating problems.

NAOMI: I Ate and Ate, and Then Made Myself Throw Up

Ten loaves of bread. Five boxes of powdered donuts. Eight boxes of various kinds of cookies. Candy bars. Bags and bags of chips. Sweet rolls. My stash. I had a secret place in the back of my closet, and I kept enough food in there to get through a nuclear blast. It made me feel good to know all that stuff was there for me. I also felt panic at the idea that something might happen to it, that someone might find it and take it away.

Whenever I had a chance, I stuffed myself with that junk. I ate and ate, and then made myself throw up. It was easy. Fill up with calories and then flush it away. A couple other girls I knew were doing the same thing. I felt like I could keep my weight down and my body in good shape while eating anything I wanted.

I was careful, though, to not stuff myself when I knew I couldn't get to a bathroom and get rid of it. So for that reason, my mom never saw me overeat, and in fact she thought I wasn't eating enough because I'd hold back at mealtimes. I raided the kitchen, of course, but I was careful not to leave evidence, like a whole empty ice cream container.

I started to buy my own food and stash it so I could get at it when I wanted it, and so that Mom wouldn't wonder where the groceries were that she'd just brought home from the store. She caught me throwing up a few times, but I had a lie handy about having the flu and she bought it, at least in the beginning. It amazes me, I guess, how easy it was for me to lie to her. It didn't bother me a bit, as long as lying helped me cover my bingeing and purging.

I got to the point where my throat hurt and all I could think about was eating, throwing up, and how fat my body was. My mom knew something was wrong because I was so moody, and because I locked myself in my room all the time. Well, one day while I was at school, she found my food stash. She confronted me with it when I got home. I of course lied and lied and lied, but she didn't buy it.

My mom got on the phone over the next several days and called anyone who had anything to do with eating problems. She learned all she could, and while she was doing that, I was mad and scared at the same time. She made me see a counselor who got me into an outpatient treatment program. And that's where I'm at now.

It's been almost two weeks since I binged, and you better believe I'm counting every minute. It's like I feel relieved that it's out in the open, but I just can't imagine ever really letting go of doing that. I get a high feeling, like a rush, when I'm bingeing. I hope I can find other ways of feeling like that without using food to do it, but I don't know. . . .

I'll have to take it one day at a time, I guess.

Eating Can Be a Disorder

How can eating become a disorder? After all, you have to eat to live. But recent studies have turned up some interesting facts about girls and eating. In her book, *Reviving Ophelia,* Mary Pipher, Ph.D., notes that "on any given day in America, half our teenage girls are dieting and one in five young women has an eating disorder." When you have an eating disorder, you're so aware of eating habits and how eating affects your body that it gets in the way of everyday living.

Eating can become a problem when food and weight become an obsession. When you're obsessed with food, you focus a great deal of attention on it—so much attention that it interferes with other areas of your life. In other words, food begins to take control of you. A food obsession often goes hand-in-hand with misperceptions about how you look, whether your weight is normal, the relationship between your eating habits and the way your body looks, and how others perceive you.

OH, NO THANKS. I'LL EAT TOMORROW!

The three specific types of eating disorders are: *Anorexia nervosa* (anorexia, for short), *Bulimia nervosa* (bulimia, for short), and compulsive overeating.* Each of these disorders has certain traits that you might recognize in yourself or someone else (the next section, pages 90–106, describes these traits). Girls who have one of these disorders also share common behaviors, including secretiveness and an abnormal emphasis on eating, food, and body shape.

"I decided to stop letting food control my life because I wanted to be happy with myself. I realized I didn't have to impress people."
Kristina, 16

---

* Another is *Eating Disorder Not Otherwise Specified,* or disorders of eating that don't meet the criteria for any specific eating disorder. For example, a girl may have all the signs of anorexia except that her weight may be in the normal range. Or a girl may meet the criteria of having bulimia, except that she binge eats less than twice a week instead of more regularly. For the purposes of this book, we're focusing our discussion on bulimia, anorexia, and compulsive overeating.

Eating disorders can cause serious, irreversible health problems, and even death. Problems with eating can also affect other areas of your life. For example, the more you fixate on food, the less energy you have for pursuing other interests such as friends, family, good grades, and outside activities. You may find that your friends change, your relationships at home get rocky, your grades drop, and your activities decrease as you spend most of your time and energy on food and weight loss. Getting help with an eating disorder involves learning about nutrition and health issues, understanding and correcting your mistaken beliefs, and finding ways to get your life back on track. This helps put *you* back in control.

Bulimia

"I'm working on not throwing up every day. I've made it for five days in a row. I'm taking it one day at a time."
Meredith, 13

Bulimia is an eating disorder that involves eating too much, called *binge eating,* and then getting rid of the food, called *purging.* We all pig out once in a while, but binge eating isn't just pigging out. Bingeing means eating large amounts of food without being able to stop and feeling out of control while doing so. A binge may be over in a few minutes, or it might last several hours, during which the person can consume thousands of calories.

Once a young woman with bulimia has consumed all this food, she will then do one of several things to rid herself of it. She might purge by making herself throw up, use laxatives and diuretics, exercise strenuously, go on a fast (not eat at all), or start an extreme diet. One way or another, she finds a way to purge the food from her system.

SARAH: I Felt Relief After Throwing Up

My dream in life was to be a model. When I was in fifth grade, I told all my friends about my modeling ambition, over and over again. One day in the middle of the school year, my two best friends just stopped talking to me. For four months, they refused to speak to me but sent notes instead. The notes said stuff like, "You're fat and ugly—how could you think you could be a model?" They even told other students to come up to me and call me names. It made me feel totally ugly.

That's when the self-hate started. In fourth grade, I thought I was pretty and I wore bikinis all the time. But by seventh grade, I believed what these girls were saying. I started to make myself throw up. I hated how I looked. I thought I had fat ankles, thick thighs, a big rear end, ugly hair, and big boobs. I felt relief after throwing up.

Well, my sister was concerned about me, so she told a school counselor who called me into her office. She got my mother involved, and I got some help. I'm now working with a counselor and a nutritionist to help me learn how to eat again. It's been hard work learning to face my feelings and accept who I am, but I'm getting better. I'm starting to eat three meals a day and exercise within reason. Although I still want to have a Barbie doll figure, I don't binge and purge. I'm getting a lot better.

And those two girls? Well, now they act like nothing happened. I even apologized to *them* at one point because I wanted to be their friend! Now they just say, "We had our reasons." When I pressed one of them for a reason, you know what she told me? She said she got mad at me because I wore the same shoes as she wore one day. Do you know what? They aren't my friends anymore.

Portrait of a Girl with Bulimia

Suppose that you're presented with a line-up of your friends and told that one of them suffers from bulimia. You're asked to pick that person from the line-up. You might have a very hard time choosing the right friend. Generally, those who develop bulimia are young women who appear healthy and are of normal weight. However, if you could look inside each friend in the line-up, you'd be able to pick out the girl struggling with bulimia. You might see these traits, *all in the extreme:*

- To her, food, weight, dieting, and body appearance are top priority.
- Being accepted by others is a prime concern.
- She feels deeply inadequate in relationships and has trouble talking about feelings.
- Although outwardly assured, she lacks confidence and self-esteem. She's very self-critical.
- She feels sad and frustrated beyond the normal ups and downs that other girls experience and are able to resolve.

"I don't compare myself to others. I am who I am, and I'm not fat."
Meg, 16

Many young women experience several or all of these problems at some time. But a girl with bulimia experiences these problems more deeply, to the point of interfering with her social, school, and family life.

How Bulimia Can Start

Deeply rooted in our culture is a fear of fat, and many of us have a powerful, learned prejudice against being overweight. In movies and magazines, on billboards and TV, just about everywhere you look, you'll see images of thin, smiling women. These images can leave a strong impression, making you feel that you have to look the same way for people to accept or admire you. Messages about the need to be thin, healthy, and fit lead many girls and young women to begin diet and exercise programs.

Starting an exercise program or fixating on eating only healthful foods can be the beginning of an eating disorder such as bulimia. Exercise and good food are, of course, important. But when you step over the line into fixating on these things, you may be heading for trouble. Eating disorders can sneak up on you. You may start out just trying to lose a little weight but quickly find yourself in a cycle of bingeing and purging.

Here's how bulimia can get started and some of the things that can happen along the way:

1. You react to emotional stress such as anxiety, anger, loneliness, or sadness by overeating and you gain weight.

2. You begin a diet, which leads to hunger and cravings.

3. You binge eat to satisfy your cravings.

4. You gain weight, which leads to feelings of guilt and fear.

5. Purging seems to be the ideal answer to avoid gaining more weight.

6. The habit of bingeing and purging becomes a routine part of every day.

7. You limit social interactions so you can hide your eating patterns. As a result, you feel isolated, lonely, and ashamed.

8. You learn to relieve these bad feelings by eating more food.

"Everyone is an individual. Some are big, some are little. Don't obsess on losing weight—you look good the way you are."
Kay, 16

Bulimia Leads to Physical Problems

Bulimia can begin as an emotional problem, but it leads to physical problems such as:

- destruction of tooth enamel, which can cause severe tooth decay, gum damage, and eventual tooth loss,
- broken blood vessels and swollen glands,
- bulging eyes and a puffy face,
- irregular or no menstrual periods,
- irregular heartbeat due to an imbalance in body fluids, which can lead to heart failure and death,
- weakness and fatigue,
- digestive problems such as nausea, bloating, stomach cramps, diarrhea, colitis (inflamed intestines), and ulcers, which can lead to partial intestine removal and/or stomach rupture (this is fatal),
- swollen, infected salivary glands (the glands that aid in swallowing and digestion),
- sore throat and pain, perforation, or bleeding of the esophagus (the tube that carries food to the stomach),
- damage to the liver and kidneys, and
- diabetes.

Signs of Bulimia

If you're bingeing and purging, or using diuretics and/or laxatives to get rid of the food you eat, you might have bulimia. Here are some warning signs of bulimia:

- episodes of binge eating,
- sense of lack of control over eating,
- bingeing and purging regularly,
- abuse of laxatives, diuretics, or diet pills,

- extremes in dieting and exercise,
- secrecy (such as eating alone),
- weight fluctuations,
- depression, isolation, or suicide attempts,
- change in appearance, including dry skin, rashes, or changes in fingernails and hair,
- swollen cheeks and neck, and
- preoccupation with dieting, weight, and food.

Anorexia

Anorexia is an eating disorder that involves self-imposed starvation. A person suffering from anorexia firmly refuses to eat even though she's extremely thin. Her fear of being fat is totally out of sync with her actual weight. In other words, she does not have the correct view of her body weight, and she's preoccupied with the size of her body. Girls with anorexia eat very little, make up excuses to avoid food, and/or refuse to eat at all. Sometimes they will binge and purge; they may also abuse laxatives, diuretics, or diet pills. And they can be thin as a needle, but something in their brain relentlessly tells them, "You're fat, you're fat, you're fat."

KERRY: Eating Almost Nothing for Days Was a Point of Pride

Everyone thought I was just a health nut. I ran two to four miles every day and exercised all the time. I "watched what I ate," which is what I told everyone when I passed up food. What no one realized was that I wasn't eating at all—or at least I ate as little as I possibly could.

It became a game with me, this eating the bare minimum. Eating almost nothing for days was a point of pride. Other girls kind of looked up to me, thinking it was way cool and almost super-disciplined of me to pass up food that they couldn't keep their hands off of. I even felt smug many times when my girlfriends said something like, "Well, look at Kerry, she's skinny as a stick."

People think girls with bulimia are the ones who obsess on food all the time. What they don't realize is that girls with anorexia focus on food just as much, only we don't eat it. All I thought about was "fat free." I read food labels closely for calories and fat, and passed up anything with either of those things. I drank water or anything with no calories.

I got so skinny that my parents finally figured out what was going on. They didn't even give me time to object—they just drove me to see a counselor at an eating disorders clinic. I was scared to meet the counselor, and mad, too. I didn't even want to tell her my name. After three visits, though, I realized my parents weren't going to back down, so I started to pretend to cooperate. Eventually, I realized the counselor really did care about me and wanted me to get better. It took a long time, but I finally decided I could trust my counselor. She didn't tell my parents what we were talking about. I managed to get the help I needed.

I'm back now. I feel better, but I also feel totally strange. Like I've got a new life, but the old habits still have a strong pull. Now I wake up each morning and plan my food for the day. Simple as it might sound to you, eating three balanced meals a day seems like a gigantic task.

If I were to advise another girl who's stepping over that line into anorexic eating, I'd tell her, "Keep yourself busy. Don't let yourself be bored, don't isolate yourself, keep occupied, always have something to do, even if you hate it! And get yourself assessed for depression."

Portrait of a Girl with Anorexia

Anorexia mainly affects white, upper- to middle-class females. But girls and women of all socioeconomic, ethnic, and racial backgrounds can develop anorexia (as well as boys and men). Anorexia is often easier to recognize than bulimia, because a girl will appear extremely thin. But if you were asked to pick out a friend in a line-up who suffers from anorexia—based only on how she behaves and *not on her physical appearance*—you might have a hard time doing so. Girls with anorexia are generally model teens—well-behaved, high achievers, eager to please. They rarely admit or complain that anything is wrong. They are often perfectionists, too. But deep inside, they may have very low self-esteem, anxiety, and feelings associated with depression.

If you could see into the minds of your friends, you'd immediately be able to pick out the one struggling with anorexia. Inside, she may be all of these things *in the extreme:*

- insecure,
- self-critical,
- overly concerned about what others think of her,
- not very tolerant,
- concerned about doing everything right,
- rigid in her thinking and judgments, and
- perfectionistic.

Interestingly, girls struggling with anorexia fixate on food just as much as girls with bulimia do—they just don't eat. As they lose more and more weight, they remain convinced that they are fat and need to keep dieting. Some girls with anorexia take pride in the fact that they get by on so little food. It becomes a kind of competition to eat as little as possible for as long as possible, as though starving themselves day by day can be marked as an achievement.

How Anorexia Can Start

Anorexia often begins with a diet started after a change of life like puberty, a relationship breakup, a death in the family, starting a new school, etc. But anorexia doesn't always start with a big trauma. Often, all it takes is a strong desire to be thin and the start of a diet and exercise program. The diet makes you feel in control: You feel you can be successful, and that makes you feel good. Then you may start exercising too much. You eat less and less, often refusing food altogether. Malnutrition and weight loss follow, which affect both your body and your mind.

ABBIE: I Eliminated as Much Fat and Sodium from My Diet as Possible

I'm 15, and my cousin is 17. We live close to each other, and we're just like sisters. I really look up to my cousin because she's a star cross-country and track runner—and she looks great! She's very conscious of what she puts into her body and runs several miles a day all year.

In the spring of last year, I found out I had made the competitive dance team at my high school. I was really excited. I wanted to be healthy like my cousin and get into great shape. So I started watching the fat, salt, and calorie content of everything I ate. That summer, we practiced two to three hours a day, five days a week. I also started running with my cousin on weekends. It was exhausting, but I didn't stop there. I eliminated as much fat and sodium from my diet as possible.

One day, my cousin and I were at a friend's softball game and I began to feel weird. The softball diamond and the players began spinning around me. I collapsed on the ground and started to have convulsions. By now I was unconscious, so the rest of the story is what my cousin told me.

My cousin started screaming, and the coaches ran over. They called 911 while my cousin called my parents. I was rushed to the hospital with everyone thinking I had epilepsy or some other brain problem. In the hospital, after many brain function tests, they found out the chemicals in my body were all out of balance. My electrolytes were way out of whack. Know what did it? Eating no fats or sodium and exercising so much.

I now know that our bodies, especially in puberty, require some fats and sodium. I spent several hours during my stay in the hospital learning what a balanced diet consists of and talking with a counselor. I'm on my way to taking better care of myself.

Anorexia Leads to Physical Problems

"You can't be a toothpick. You've got to have some meat on your bones."

Tanya, 18

As with bulimia, anorexia leads to physical problems such as:

- pale complexion (a pasty look), bruising,
- shrinkage of internal organs, especially the kidneys, heart, and brain,
- irregular heart rhythm and congestive heart failure,
- changes in body chemistry, which cause other heart problems,
- irregular or no menstrual periods,
- possible loss of ability to have children,
- weakness, fatigue, and/or fainting spells,
- bowel, urinary, and digestive problems,
- muscle cramps and aches, swelling of joints,
- nerve and tendon injuries,
- inability to concentrate, headaches,
- loss of hair on the head, but growth of fine body hair elsewhere, such as the face and stomach, and
- possible early start of osteoporosis (weakening of bones).

Signs of Anorexia

Following are some warning signs of anorexia. Watch for these changes in yourself or a friend:

- excessive weight loss, even as much as 25 percent over several months,

- damage to teeth and gums,
- dull, stringy hair or loss of hair,
- brittle nails and dry skin,
- absence of menstrual periods,
- tendency to wear baggy clothes to hide body,
- sensitivity to cold (due to loss of fat and muscle tissue),
- growth of fine hair on body and face,
- excessive exercise to burn calories,
- overuse of diet pills, laxatives, and/or diuretics,
- withdrawal from family and friends to concentrate on weight,
- lack of self-confidence,
- unrealistic body image (feeling fat despite being thin), and
- unusual eating habits, including a preoccupation with dieting or secretiveness about food.

If you suspect a friend may have anorexia, take a look at her eating habits next time you're with her at dinner or in the lunchroom. Following are some clues to watch for. She may:

- show up late or not at all,
- fail to eat,
- eat a very small amount,
- eat extremely slowly,
- cut food into tiny pieces,
- push her food around the plate aimlessly,
- consume lots of low-calorie vegetables or noncaloric condiments,
- throw away large portions of uneaten food, and/or
- secretly discard her food when she thinks others aren't looking.

Compulsive Overeating

A girl with compulsive overeating disorder, also called *binge eating disorder*, binges but doesn't purge. Or she just eats a lot but doesn't try to get rid of the food. The result? You guessed it—obesity. Compulsive overeaters are often constantly dieting. They get caught up in a cycle where they:

1. overeat,
2. gain weight,
3. diet to lose weight,
4. feel miserable while dieting,
5. break the diet and feel guilty about it,

6. find relief and comfort in eating,

7. gain back any weight that was lost, plus some, and

8. diet again.

Like bulimia and anorexia, compulsive overeating narrows a girl's world. Her energy, thoughts, and attention are completely absorbed with eating and food. She pulls away from other people, activities, events, and interests. At a time of life when the world is a place to be explored, a teenage girl suffering from compulsive overeating misses out on important life experiences.

ERICA: I Ate Whatever I Could Get My Hands On

Talk about a food obsession, I had it. I ate whatever I could get my hands on. I ate fast, without even tasting the food, and as soon as I was done, I planned what else I was going to eat. In between overeating spells, I went on crash diets. Any diet I heard or read about, I tried. I got caught in this little game or cycle of dieting, and then rewarding myself with food for doing such a great job with my dieting.

Besides eating a lot, I hid food. I bought or took extra of everything you can imagine and hid it all over my room and the house. Food was always there for me. I ate when my boyfriend broke up with me. I ate when things went right, and I ate when things went wrong.

I gained so much weight, in spite of dieting constantly, that I couldn't stand myself. And because I was fat, I hated myself. And because I hated myself, I ate. You get the picture. There's no end to it.

Then, one day, I was getting a checkup by my doctor. She asked me to tell her about eating and my weight, etc. I was shocked, and I felt ashamed right away. I can remember feeling my ears burn and my cheeks flush as I tried to explain away my weight. The doctor was smart enough to just wave all that aside. She kept asking me questions until finally I admitted I needed help with overeating.

After that, things moved fast. My doctor helped me figure out what overeating all the time was doing to me. She got me into a treatment program. Now I plan each meal, and I make sure I eat something three times a day. The weird thing is that, now that I'm actually eating three meals a day, I'm losing weight. Go figure.

I just wish my problem wasn't food, because you *have to* eat. At least with other stuff like smoking, you can quit and walk away from the thing—your body doesn't need it to survive. But I have to eat. So I have to plan it, think ahead, and try not to eat for reasons like being depressed, or getting a bad grade, or feeling ugly, or responding to put-downs. I'm trying to teach myself to eat to feed my body—not to cover a bad feeling, or to get that sugar rush and feel high for a short time. Food is the fuel for my body, not my mind.

I used to think I'd never make it, never be able to change being a compulsive overeater. And I couldn't do it when I thought about curbing it for my whole life. I joined a support group so I wouldn't have to do it alone. My doctor told me to just do it a day at a time. And that's what I do. I wake up and plan my food for that day before I ever get out of bed. What I know now is that if I work at it just for this minute, I can do it.

Portrait of a Compulsive Overeater

Compulsive overeating results in obesity, which carries with it a host of physical problems—many of them quite serious. But along the way, compulsive overeaters do a lot of dieting. The constant dieting, which may involve shedding ten, twenty, thirty, or more pounds followed by regaining the weight, messes up your metabolism.

Almost anyone can become a compulsive overeater. In our culture, food is often connected with nurturing and warmth. It's a key part of our holidays, family gatherings, social events, dates, proms, and parties. Food makes us feel good: It has both an emotional and a chemical power. The compulsive overeater learns to connect food with feeling better.

In a line-up of your friends, if you had to pick the one with compulsive overeating disorder based only on how she behaves and *not on her physical appearance*, you'd want to look for the girl who:

"Looks don't matter as much as a good attitude."
Mary, 17

- tends to take care of others,
- diets constantly,
- breaks the diet with episodes of overeating,
- is obsessed with calories and weight, and
- deals with her feelings by eating.

The compulsive overeater in the group will be the one who eats when she's mad, lonely, tired, fearful, or stressed out.

How Compulsive Overeating Can Start

The compulsive overeating cycle begins with eating to cover feelings or to feel better. Extra eating leads to weight gain, which leads to crash dieting. But often the diet makes a girl who's a compulsive overeater feel irritable, deprived, and miserable again, so she eats to feel better. Weight loss becomes associated with being in control and weight gain with being out of control. The cycle goes on and on, resulting in the young woman focusing too much time and attention on eating or not eating.

Compulsive Overeating Leads to Physical Problems

"I think stress, anxiety, and pressure from society have a lot to do with eating disorders."
Susan, 14

Compulsive overeating often involves a cycle of gaining and losing weight, which is hard on the body. It can start out as an emotional problem but leads to physical problems such as:

- obesity, which can lead to further health problems (diabetes, heart disease, etc.),
- slow metabolism, leading to sluggishness or sleepiness,
- increased risk of heart and respiratory problems,
- circulatory problems, and
- high blood pressure.

Signs of Compulsive Overeating

If you're struggling with a cycle of overeating and dieting, you may be in danger of becoming a compulsive overeater. Here are some warning signs of compulsive overeating:

- repeated dieting,
- obsession with calories and weight loss,
- eating to ease emotional pain,
- eating to cover other feelings, and
- obesity.

Body Image: A Key Issue

At the heart of all three of these eating disorders is one key issue: body image. You may think you know what you look like, but your picture of yourself probably doesn't match reality.

What's in a body image? Everything, when it comes to eating disorders. The connection is simple: What you think your body looks like determines how you eat. The interesting fact about girls who suffer from eating disorders is this: *They don't correctly perceive how they look. Their sense of their own body shape is simply wrong. But they* believe *their misperception.*

How does this happen? It's really a combination of factors. For example, a girl going through puberty may

feel insecure about her changing body. As she pages through a fashion magazine or watches TV, the articles and ads tell her that being thin is "in." This may lead her to start a diet, and that first diet is often enough to begin the eating disorder cycle. Achieving the "perfect" body is a multi-million-dollar industry (aimed primarily at girls and women) involving fitness, cosmetics, and diet programs. Many girls and young women end up measuring themselves against the unrealistic ideals offered by the media. The result? A negative body image.

"People like you for you. Don't allow other people to affect the way you think about yourself."
Laura, 17

Many girls grow up believing that living up to society's ideal of beauty or physical attractiveness is necessary to succeed, be popular, have friends, and attract boyfriends. As a result, girls can become obsessed with appearance: clothing, skin, hair, makeup, jewelry, mannerisms, and especially weight and body size. In addition, certain professions and activities common to women emphasize fitness, weight, size, and shape. For instance, dancers, actresses, athletes, models, and gymnasts often fixate on their weight and physical appearance, leaving them vulnerable to developing an eating disorder.

But there's something terribly important you need to know about this national fixation with being thin: It's a sham. Human beings—living, breathing girls and women—aren't meant to look like Barbie dolls. Barbie isn't the real thing. She's plastic, molded on a factory assembly line. Living, breathing females do not have, never have had, and never will have a body shape that looks exactly like Barbie, at least not without considerable surgical help. (We're talking liposuction, implants, lots of stitches, and pain. Is it worth it?)

When your ideal of what you should look like is based on Barbie or runway models, and when your image of yourself is dependent on feedback you get from other people, you could be heading for trouble. Set realistic standards for yourself when it comes to your appearance, and don't rely on other people for approval. Keep in mind that not liking how you look can be a sign of a deeper problem: not liking who you are. Try to feel good about yourself—how you look and who you are, inside and outside. You can do this by taking good care of yourself: Eat healthful foods, don't go on crash diets, stay active, and avoid smoking, drinking, and taking drugs.

Also, be aware that gaining weight and adding body fat is a normal part of growing up. Your body's doing what it's supposed to be doing. How much you weigh and how your body is shaped is predetermined by your genes, and you can't alter your genetic make-up no matter how hard you try.

Reality Check

Following are some myths and reality checks about food and eating disorders.

⊗ **Myth** If I don't eat, I'm in control of myself and my life.

⊕ **Reality check** If you don't allow yourself to eat, it's likely that food or an eating disorder is controlling you.

⊗ **Myth** Only girls and young women get eating disorders.

⊕ **Reality check** Eating disorders are on the rise among boys and men. Older women can have eating disorders, too.

⊗ **Myth** It won't hurt me to not eat for a while to lose weight or stay thin.

⊕ **Reality check** Not eating simply isn't healthy—your body needs food to keep it going. Not eating can become a bad habit and is a sign of anorexia.

⊗ **Myth** It's okay to want to be as thin as a model, because models represent the true ideal of female beauty.

⊕ **Reality check** The average model weighs about 23 percent less than the average woman. According to medical standards, most models weigh too little for their body size and may fit the profile of having anorexia.

⊗ **Myth** Girls who diet, who binge and purge, or who don't eat are just trying to make themselves look better.

⊕ **Reality check** Many girls have the wrong idea about how they should—or even can—look. Dieting, starving, or bingeing and purging can, over time, make someone look a lot worse.

The first step in moving beyond an eating disorder is recognizing that you might have one. If you think you have bulimia, anorexia, or compulsive overeating disorder (or if you suspect a friend might), it's very important to talk to an adult who knows about eating disorders. Contact your doctor, a counselor, an eating disorders support group leader, a school social worker, or other person who can offer expert help and advice. See pages 119–121 in the next chapter for info lines and Web sites that can also offer information and support.

7

Seeing the Problem and Getting Help

There's something that all eating disorders have in common: secrecy. Whether a girl is suffering from anorexia, bulimia, or compulsive overeating, she's probably suffering alone. Every day, she might hide food in her secret stash; hide her weight beneath big clothes; hide the fact that she's dieting, fasting, purging, or exercising too much; or hide from the world to concentrate on eating and her weight.

The key to overcoming an eating disorder is first recognizing, then admitting, you have one. *You don't have to face it alone.* The physical and emotional problems of eating disorders can take a terrible toll on you, and you'll need the help of an expert to regain control of your eating habits and your life. This chapter tells you how and where to find the help you need.

If you're worried about a friend who might have an eating disorder, talk to her and to an adult who can offer help and guidance. See pages 112–114, "Helping a Friend," for information about what you can do for a friend with an eating disorder, and pages 119–121, "Finding Resources," to learn about helpful organizations and Web sites.

"I didn't take my anorexia support group seriously until one of the members leaned toward me and said, 'No one likes the look of a skeletal body.' It made me think harder about what I was doing to myself."
Aliana, 15

Identifying an Eating Disorder

If you need help figuring out if you or a friend might have an eating disorder, read through the list below to recognize the key signs. (For more details about these disorders, see the previous chapter, pages 86–110.)

Someone with an eating disorder might:

- fixate on food, calories, eating, dieting, weight, and body shape,
- feel fat no matter how much weight is lost,
- diet or exercise excessively,
- eat alone, or hide eating and food, or hide weight gain or loss,
- eat large amounts of food in a short time,
- purge after eating,
- strive to do things perfectly and be perfect,
- withdraw from friends or family,
- feel guilty after eating,
- feel afraid of gaining weight,
- hoard food, and/or
- spend a lot of time in the bathroom after eating.

If you see several of these signs in yourself, turn to page 119 and read "Finding Resources." If you recognize these signs in a friend, read the next section, "Helping a Friend."

Helping a Friend

If a friend of yours is struggling with an eating disorder, she needs expert help. You don't have to handle the situation alone: Contact a doctor, parent, school counselor, school nurse, coach, clergy member, or other adult who can find the expert help your friend needs. (NOTE: If your friend is doing something that scares you, tell an adult you trust *right away.* For example, bingeing and purging, complaining of constant or severe stomach pain, or talking about suicide are clues to get *immediate* help.) You can also get help and information from the info lines and Web sites listed on pages 119–121.

Let your friend know that she has your support. Below are some suggestions for talking to a friend about eating disorders.

- Tell her you care and that you'd like her to get help. Make specific suggestions about adults she can talk to. Let her know that she shouldn't feel ashamed or guilty about her eating disorder.

- Make sure your friend knows you understand this: *The eating disorder is the problem—she isn't the problem.*

- Share what you know about eating disorders. Tell her how you think the eating disorder has affected her, you, her other friends, and her family.

- Share your problems. Let your friend know that you're human, too.

- Ask her what she thinks. Listen to her.

- Know that when you talk to your friend, she may respond with anger. Or she may deny what you've said. This reaction may be due to her fear of being found out, shame, or a number of other strong emotions. Just persist and try to help. Understand, too, that you can only do so much. *Do not* blame yourself if your friend refuses to get help.

Because your friend is probably going through a difficult struggle, it can be helpful for you to know what *not* to say in daily conversations with her. Some statements, while not intended to be hurtful, can affect someone with an eating disorder very deeply. For example, don't say:

1. *"All this dieting is making you look awful."*
   Because a girl with an eating disorder is overly concerned with her appearance, don't make any negative comments about how she looks.

2. *"Can't you just eat like the rest of us?"*
   Remember that your friend is dealing with difficult emotional issues that affect her eating. A comment like this may make her feel more guilty and out of control.

3. *"Hey, you finally put on a little weight! You look great."*
   She won't hear the "looks great" part. She'll only hear that she's put on weight.

4. *"Have you been puking again?"*
   Purging usually causes girls with eating disorders a great deal of guilt. Your friend will probably feel even more ashamed after a comment like this.

5. *"If you think you're fat, you probably think I'm huge."*
   Eating disorders cause a girl to have a distorted view of her body and weight—a view that doesn't extend to other people. Try not to mention weight around someone with an eating disorder.

6. *"I wish I had your problem because I'd probably be a lot thinner."*
   Your friend knows how hard it is to deal with eating problems, and she wouldn't want to see you go through what she's going through. Don't minimize her problem.

7. *"How can you do this to your friends and family?"*
   A comment like this will probably make your friend feel worse. She may respond by withdrawing even further.

Avoiding Eating Problems

Eating disorders sap the vitality and contribution of many young women at a time when they could be experiencing what the world has to offer. A little knowledge about how you eat and the role food plays can prevent food from taking control of your life. Here are nine ways to maintain healthy attitudes about eating, weight, your body, and yourself.

1. *Take care of your body.*
   Eat regular, nutritious meals each day.
2. *Eat a variety of things in reasonable portions.*
   Use a plate, sit down, and don't do other things like watch TV or read while eating. Eat slowly.
3. *Exercise or be physically active, especially in sports or activities you enjoy.*
   When you exercise, don't do it just to burn fat. Do it because it makes you feel good.

4. *Be aware of your feelings.*
   Pay attention to your feelings, rather than ignore them.

5. *Take charge of your life.*
   Make choices that lead to feeling balanced. Trust your decisions.

6. *Take care of your mind.*
   The more you know, the more you feel in control. Be a sponge. Learn and absorb everything. Nurture your curiosity. Build successes in school.

7. *Take care of your social life.*
   Don't isolate yourself. Make friends by being a friend, not by pleasing others. Find friends who like you because of your unique personality.

8. *Take care of your body image.*
   Be alert to social pressures to be thin; recognize society's subtle messages that "you are what you weigh."

9. *Learn to look at yourself in a full-length mirror.*
   Make an accurate mental picture of your body shape, and counter negative messages with the truth: *There is no single perfect body image or type.* Bodies simply house who we are—our personality, emotions, thoughts, values. Every body is as unique and special as the person who inhabits it.

"It doesn't matter what other people think— learn to be happy with yourself."
Angela, 16

MICHELE: I Do a Lot of Things Now to Try to Keep Food and Eating in Balance

I'm on the other end of the eating problems, now . . . at least I think I'm better. I was bingeing and purging lots of times all day long. I stopped when two friends of mine told Mrs. Adams, our school social worker. She called me in, and after I spent an hour denying everything, I finally told her the truth. My parents helped out, and I went through a treatment program that helped a lot, but not at first. It took me a couple of months before I decided to do the program.

I do a lot of things now to try to keep food and eating in balance. I run, which also helps my depression, and a nutritionist worked out an eating plan for me so I know exactly what I'm going to eat each day. That helps a lot because I really don't have to think about eating. I've also tried yoga to help me stay focused . . . sometimes I feel like I'm flying apart, going in all directions at once, and then I don't think clearly.

What I'd like to tell other girls to help them avoid going through the junk I've been through is: "Balance everything in your life." I even work to keep my running in balance, so I don't start obsessing or overdoing that. Don't overdo anything. A counselor taught me one thing I try to remember. She said, "Honor your body and your body's need for nutrition." She said that means to think of food not as pleasure, or entertainment, or something to obsess on—but as fuel. I try to remember that whenever I'm struggling with food.

Getting Help

Getting help for an eating disorder often involves treatment or seeing a counselor. Treatment may take place at a small clinic or in a hospital. During treatment, you might end up staying overnight or for an extended period of time, and you may work with individual counselors or with groups of people who are struggling with the same problems you are.

The idea of treatment or counseling may make you feel afraid and angry. It's normal to fear something unfamiliar—change can be scary. But give treatment a good chance: Think of it not as a punishment, but as an opportunity. You'll come out of treatment stronger than when you went in.

"One thing I learned in treatment for my bulimia is that it's really hard not to care about what you look like, but other people truly don't think about it as much as you do. I remind myself of that lots of times each day."
Melinda, 15

117

What Happens During Treatment

Treatment for bulimia might involve:

- a medical evaluation,
- individual counseling,
- family therapy,
- group work,
- hospitalization if physical complications are involved,
- exercise and meal planning, and/or
- nutrition counseling.

Treatment for anorexia might involve:

- a medical evaluation,
- individual counseling,
- family therapy,
- hospitalization if physical problems develop,
- exercise and meal planning, and/or
- relaxation and biofeedback techniques.

Treatment for compulsive overeating might involve:

- a medical evaluation,
- individual counseling,
- family therapy,
- a nutrition plan,
- an exercise program with a personal trainer,
- a support group for help if you're feeling discouraged.

All of this may sound overwhelming, so keep this in mind as you go through the healing process: You can take it one step at a time, and you'll have help every step of the way.

Finding Resources

The first step toward getting the professional help you need is talking to an adult you trust who knows what eating disorders are. Tell a parent, doctor, teacher, coach, school nurse, clergy member, or another adult you think will listen, understand, and find you some professional help. You can also contact support groups or eating disorder clinics in your community. Check the Yellow Pages under "Eating Disorders" to find programs that are available. For help with compulsive overeating disorder, you can look under "Overeaters Anonymous" in your phone book. When you call, ask where a group meets in your area.

If you're looking for other resources, you can call an info line or explore the World Wide Web. Some numbers and sites are listed below.

Info Lines

These numbers aren't toll-free, so they'll show up on your phone bill.

- (212) 501-8351 is the number for the American Anorexia/Bulimia Association in New York. They are available Monday through Friday 9 A.M. to 5 P.M. EST to give you information and to tell you where to find clinics, counselors, and support groups in your area.

- (847) 831-3438 connects you to the National Association of Anorexia Nervosa and Associated Disorders (ANAD). You can reach them Monday through Friday 9 A.M. to 5 P.M. CST. ANAD provides free information about eating disorders, phone counseling, and referrals to counselors and self-help groups in your area.

119

- (505) 891-2664 is the number for the World Service office of Overeaters Anonymous. You can call Monday through Friday 8 A.M. to 5 P.M. MST for information on this 12-step group. The program helps overeaters, as well as those with anorexia or bulimia.

Web Sites

To explore these sites, you'll need access to a computer and the Internet.

- Something Fishy
  http://www.something-fishy.com
  This excellent site is one part of EDSA (Eating Disorders Shared Awareness), a group started by two women who have eating disorders, to link helpful online resources for people with eating disorders. Something Fishy has tons of information about eating disorders and related issues, personal stories from girls and women, a chat room where you can "talk" with other people who have eating disorders, how and where to get help for you or a friend, links to many other sites, and much more—all presented in a friendly, caring style, with fun graphics.

- Eating Disorders
  http://icewall.vianet.on.ca/pages/colleen/eatdis.htm
  Sponsored by Colleen Thompson, a founding member of EDSA (see above), this site also has loads of information about signs and symptoms to watch for, suggestions for how to approach someone you think has an eating disorder, how to take good care of yourself, special issues related to eating disorders, how to find help, words of hope, links to other sites, and much more—also presented in a friendly, comforting tone, with appealing graphics.

- Cath's Links to Eating Disorders Resources on the Net
  http://www.stud.unit.no/studorg/ikstrh/ed/
  Started by Catherine Sundnes, a woman with anorexia, this site provides links to other sites with lots of information about eating disorders, resources, and how to find help for you or a friend.

- Mental Health Net
  http://www.cmhc.com/selfhelp.htm
  This site has links to thousands of online self-help resources on a wide variety of health issues, including eating disorders. Each site listed is rated by the staff, based on quality of content and presentation, making this site especially helpful and easy to use.

"I'd like to be someone who doesn't give in to peer pressure,

someone who stands up for what she feels is right.

A person who can say no."

Pamela, 15

Taking Charge

of *Your Mind & Body:*
Steps for

Positive Change

Introduction to Part Four

Why You Need to Read This

If you've read the first three parts of this book, you know some of the problems that girls face today. You know some of the reasons why girls might choose to use alcohol and other drugs, smoke, and become fixated on food. And you know some of the harmful effects that these choices can have on a girl's physical and mental health, relationships, and success in school and life.

We understand that it's sometimes hard to resist the peer pressure, societal pressure, mood swings, hormonal ups and downs, poor role models, shaky self-esteem, and other influences that might lead you to make unhealthy choices about what goes into your body. But we also believe that you *want* to make better choices, or you wouldn't be reading this book. And that's the whole point of Part Four.

In this part of the book, we give you proven, powerful tools you can use to learn more about yourself, get in touch with your wants and needs, and become the clear, sure, strong person you're capable of being. Not only will these tools help you to make good choices about alcohol and other drugs, food, and smoking; they will also enable you to take charge of your life in positive ways, get what you want and need, improve your relationships, and *much* more.

What you're about to read is a basic self-help "course" in communication, problem solving, relationship building, self-awareness, and self-care that will give you more control over your life than you ever thought possible. With these skills, you can start making positive changes today—*right now*—that will make a tremendous difference in every aspect of your life, for the rest of your life.

This may seem like a huge promise to make, and it is. That's why it's important for you to know that these skills have been tried and tested for years. Millions of people have learned them and used them successfully, and so can you. They're easy to learn, easy to understand, and some are so simple that you won't believe they can possibly work—until you try them and see for yourself.

8

Becoming a Better Communicator

How Mistaken Beliefs Can Affect Relationships

Unless you're a hermit, you've spent (and will spend) much of your life relating to other people. Your world will also include your parents, siblings, other relatives, teachers, classmates, neighbors, girlfriends, boyfriends, teammates, acquaintances, coworkers, employers, employees, your marriage or life partner, and perhaps your own children and *their* friends and partners and children and . . . the list is endless! For your life to be meaningful and satisfying, you need to be able to get along with many different people. This isn't something that happens naturally. It's something you *learn*.

You learn to relate to others by watching people around you, especially your parents and other important adults. You learn to communicate, solve problems, resolve conflicts, and interact with others by first observing and then interpreting what you've observed. Sometimes you don't make the best interpretation, and this leads to what psychiatrist Alfred Adler called *mistaken beliefs.*

Mistaken beliefs are formed when we're very young. For example, a toddler wants a cookie before dinner. When her mother says no, the toddler throws a tantrum. Mom is busy fixing dinner and doesn't have time to deal with a tantrum, so she gives the toddler a cookie. Somewhere below the level of conscious awareness, the toddler makes this interpretation: *When I throw a tantrum, I get what I want.*

Several days later, Mom and the toddler are outdoors when the ice cream truck comes down the street. The toddler wants ice cream, Mom says no, and the toddler throws a tantrum. Once again, Mom gives in.

From these two experiences, the toddler makes an interpretation that becomes a rule or law for her life. It goes something like this: *When I throw a tantrum, I always get what I want.* Or: *I should always get what I want, and the way to get it is by throwing a tantrum.* This rule keeps "working" for as long as adults keep reinforcing it by giving in. Eventually, adults stop tolerating the tantrums, but until then, the toddler's relationships with people will be based in part on mistaken beliefs. And if the toddler becomes a child and then a teen who still has these mistaken beliefs, she's going to have definite problems relating to others.

This is only one example of how mistaken beliefs can start. These beliefs and the rules that grow out of them can last until we're adults, unless we choose to change them. This happens when the beliefs and rules stop working, when we become aware of them, or when we decide to do things differently.

Throughout Part Four, we'll return often to the idea of mistaken beliefs. Along the way, you'll have the chance to examine some of your own mistaken beliefs. You'll learn that you have the power to keep a belief or throw it out—to change the way you respond to others, to act instead of react.

Using "I Messages"

Clear communication with your friends, parents, teachers, siblings—just about anyone in your life—can make a big difference in how well you get along with others and meet your own needs. Clear communication depends on three things:

1. not putting the other person on the defensive,
2. getting your message across, and
3. receiving the other person's message.

Using "I messages" is a great way to accomplish the first two things.

Most people tend to use "you messages" when they communicate with others, especially about problems. For example:

> "You make me so mad! I thought you were my friend, and you're over there talking and laughing with Sue, and you know I can't stand her! You don't know how to be a friend. If you really liked me, you wouldn't talk to her. You can choose either Sue or me!"

Imagine that a friend has just said this to you. Imagine how you feel. Are you willing to sit down with her, talk calmly about the problem, and work together to arrive at a solution? Probably not, because her "you messages"—"YOU make me mad, YOU don't know how to be a friend"—have put you on the defensive. Instead of thinking, "This is my friend, and I care about her," you're thinking, "What's happening? What am I going to say back? How can I get out of here? Help!" Your first priority is to protect yourself. Clear communication is impossible.

"I messages" shift the focus off of the other person ("you") and onto how the speaker ("I") is feeling. For example:

"I feel hurt and confused when I see you and Sue talking and laughing because I thought you and I were best friends, and I don't like her at all. I even wonder if you're talking about me! I'm not sure that I can trust you anymore, and what I need now is to talk to you about this."

A friend has just said this to you; how do you feel? You're probably more willing to listen because you're not under attack. And you're more likely to solve your problem together.

"I messages" don't guarantee that things will turn out exactly as you and your friend hope they will, but they do improve the chances that you'll be able to communicate clearly. If you want to try using "I messages," here's how:

1. Think about how you are feeling and why. Take your time. Remember that the point of an "I message" isn't to blame the other person, but to focus on your feelings. This means figuring out your feelings and taking responsibility for them.

2. Form your "I message" with phrases using these starter words:

   • I feel . . .

   • When . . .

   • Because . . .

   • What I need (or what I would like to see happen) is. . . .

The order of these words and phrases doesn't matter. What's important is to keep "you" out of it and use "I" whenever possible. You might also try these starters:

   • I have a problem with . . .

   • I'm concerned about . . .

   • This is how I feel when. . . .

Here's another example: Imagine that your mother is constantly nagging you about your compulsive overeating and weight. You might decide to ignore her and keep eating whenever and whatever you want, just to prove to your mother that she can't control you. Naturally, she'll be angry and hurt—but the person who will be hurt *most* by this decision is *you*. It's your body, and you're not taking good care of it.

Or you might decide to talk back to your mother and scream at her to quit nagging you. Which will only make your relationship worse.

Or you might decide to use "I messages." You could say something like this:

> "Mom, I feel embarrassed and angry when you nag me about my eating and my weight, because I feel like you're treating me like a little kid. What happens is I want to get back at you—and I end up eating more! Do you think we can talk about this and make an agreement we both can live with?"

Approaching your problem in this way opens the door to communication with your mother. It strengthens your relationship and gives you the opportunity to brainstorm solutions to your compulsive eating—such as planning your meals, starting an exercise program, meeting with a nutritionist, or seeing a doctor or counselor.

SONDRA: I Decided to Give "I Messages" a Try

I learned about "I messages" in health class three different times—in seventh grade, eighth grade, and tenth grade. We all made fun of the idea, thinking it was really stupid.

I started going with this guy, and we fought all the time. I decided (without anyone knowing) to give "I messages" a try. When I did, my boyfriend and I actually started talking instead of yelling at each other. We still have problems, but we fight a lot less than we used to. I guess maybe the idea wasn't as stupid as I originally thought.

Using Reflective Listening

Is there someone in your life with whom you argue a lot or get into power struggles? If you're locked in a stand-off with a parent, friend, or anyone else, something has to give so you both can move forward. When neither of you is willing to back off, reflective listening can help.

When you're having problems with other people, it helps to remember that *you can't change them.* People change only if they *choose* to change. What you *can* change is the way you relate and respond to them. In time, given your example, they may change the way they relate and respond to you.

With reflective listening, you choose not to dig in your heels and insist, "I'm right and you're wrong and that's all there is to it!" Instead, you listen carefully to what other people say, then frame responses that *reflect* their words—sort of like a verbal mirror. This makes it hard for them to argue with you, because how can they argue with themselves?

Reflective listening involves more than just repeating what other people say; that's being a parrot. You have to think about the *feeling* that lies behind the words. This is a skill that takes some practice.

Here's an example: Your dad is angry with you, and he yells, "You can't do anything right! Why can't you ever make the right decision? Why do you always have to go out and do the wrong things?" Instead of yelling back, you say (in a respectful way), "It sounds like you think I'm being irresponsible." He can't argue with that, because that's what he *does* think! It might take him a moment or two to settle down and stop yelling, but when he does, the two of you can have a real talk.

If you want to try using reflective listening, here's how:

1. Listen closely to what the other person is saying, and try not to get angry or defensive.
2. Listen for the feeling behind the words.
3. Take a moment to think about how you can reflect what the other person has just said.
4. Speak calmly, respectfully, and firmly, without an attitude.

You can use reflective listening in almost any situation, but it's especially helpful for solving problems or addressing conflicts. Especially if the adults in your life tend to use a "blame-and-shame" approach, reflective listening is a positive, healthy alternative.

BOBBI: I Honestly Believed This Was Crazy

I have a younger sister who's really a pain. We fight all the time over anything and everything. And guess who always gets in trouble? Me. I'm the oldest, so I'm expected to not fight with her, but I don't buy it.

My parents took me to a counselor because, in their words, "Bobbi seems so unhappy, and she's always fighting with her sister." I was so mad at them for taking me to the counselor that I wouldn't even talk to this lady. But after a few sessions, I found out that she was really okay. She taught me what she called "reflective listening." I laughed at her when she was teaching me (respectfully, of course). We role-played using it the next time my sister started in on me. I honestly believed this was crazy.

Well, the first time I tried it with my sister, I could hardly keep a straight face. But it worked! I nearly dropped dead. My sister had no one to argue with, and she just left the room. I use it now with her, and even with my parents and friends, and I have to laugh inside each time at how well it works. It sure beats yelling and screaming all the time.

Using Active Listening

Active listening is another way to promote clear communication and solve problems. When you use active listening, other people feel as if you're paying attention and really "hearing" them. You can use active listening in combination with reflective listening, because each strengthens the other.

If you want to try active listening, here's how:

1. Stop whatever else you're doing and give the other person your full attention.

2. Look at the other person.

3. Lean forward to indicate that you're listening.

4. Repeat back what you hear the other person say. (Here's where you might want to use reflective listening instead of repeating the other person's words exactly.)

5. Nod your head when you hear something you agree with.

6. Ask questions if you hear something you don't understand.

7. Stay calm and be respectful.

When you use active listening, your body language and attitude let the other person know that you're genuinely interested in what he or she has to say. Conversations tend to go more smoothly, and the results are more positive.

CARRIE: I Couldn't Believe How Great It Felt to Actually Be Heard

It seems like every time I try to talk to my mom, she's too busy to listen. She's doing dishes, picking up, reading the newspaper, doing the laundry, watching TV, or running errands. It's so frustrating!

The other day I was at my friend Donna's house, and she started to tell her mom about an incident at school we were both involved in. Her mom actually stopped cooking dinner, sat down, and listened to us. She asked us questions, and she even let the answering machine pick up a call that came in while we were talking. I mean, she sat right down at the table with us—she wasn't just stirring a pot, glancing over at us, and saying "Oh" once in a while.

I couldn't believe how great it felt to actually be *heard*. I think I'll try telling my mom about this—if I can get her to stop what she's doing for a minute to listen to me.

If you want to communicate clearly, solve problems, avoid conflicts, and stop arguments in their tracks, start by being a good listener. And when you have something important to say, use "I messages."

135

9

Becoming a Better Problem Solver

Pushing Your Own Buttons

Do you like it when your parents, friends, or boyfriends try to control you? When they tell you what to do, how to think, and sometimes even how to feel? Probably not! Control issues are a major source of problems between people. In fact, *you* are in control of all your thoughts and feelings.

136

If you don't believe this, or you're not sure what it means, try this experiment:

1. Go to a quiet place where you can think and get comfortable—somewhere you're not likely to be interrupted for the next several minutes. Sit down or lie down.

2. Picture in your mind a remote control, like the one that operates a TV or VCR.

3. Now imagine that your body is a remote control that operates your mind. Figure out where and how you're going to push the buttons on your remote control—for example, by squeezing your thumb and forefinger together.

4. Close your eyes and take a few deep breaths to relax.

5. Now picture a positive experience in your life—an event that caused you to have good feelings like happiness, love, or excitement.

6. Replay that experience in your mind as if you're watching a program on TV. Relive the feelings that went along with the experience. Take your time doing this.

7. Now push a button on your remote control and change the channel to a minor negative experience—an event that produced feelings of anger, sadness, disappointment, hurt, or fear.

8. Relive that experience in your mind, and try to actually *feel* those feelings again.

9. Now push a button on your remote control and go back to the program of your positive experience. Relive the feelings associated with that experience. *Feel* them again.

10. Open your eyes.

As you did this, could you feel your emotions changing? If you could, here's why: When you pushed the button on your remote control and changed the

137

channel (your thoughts), your feelings also changed. *Thoughts trigger feelings.* Even though you were following a set of instructions that said "change the channel," *you* made the decision to actually do it. You controlled your thoughts and, therefore, your feelings. They weren't controlled by other people. You did it all by yourself.

What this means is that *other people can't control your thoughts and feelings.* You can *choose* to let them influence you, you can *choose* to think and feel the way they want you to, but they can't force you. You don't have to be a victim.

NOTE: Abusive relationships are an exception to this rule. If you are being physically, sexually, or emotionally abused, controlling your thoughts and feelings isn't enough. It's important to take *immediate* steps to end the abuse. Find an adult you trust and feel safe with, and tell him or her what's happening to you. Get help! For suggestions on finding a safe adult, see pages 182–185.

When you decide to stop being a victim, you need to start taking responsibility for your thoughts and feelings. This causes problems for some people. Sometimes it's easier to stay a victim and blame someone else for the way you feel. It's easier to say, "She made me so mad!" or "He really ticked me off!" than to think, "I *chose* to get angry, and it doesn't feel good, so I guess I'd better take control of my thoughts and stop feeling this way." In this case, easier isn't better. Why let someone else push the buttons on *your* remote control?

JODI: Possessiveness and Jealousy Were Not What I Wanted in a Relationship

I started going with Steve when I was a ninth grader. It was really fun to be with him all the time, and it felt great to have a "guy." Things were going great. Steve and I talked on the phone every night, spent time together Friday and Saturday nights, and spent Sundays hanging out at the local coffee shop.

After a while, Steve started getting irritated with me when I talked with other guys, even though they were just friends of mine. At first, I thought this was kind of neat because I thought it proved that Steve cared about me. Eventually, Steve started getting angry if I didn't spend every minute with him or if I talked to other friends. In the beginning, I got angry back, so we spent most of our time arguing and yelling at each other.

My older sister noticed I was acting down, like something was bothering me. When I told her that Steve was being really possessive and jealous, my sister talked with me about control and relationships. I decided that possessiveness and jealousy were not what I wanted in a relationship, so I chose to not allow Steve to upset me anymore. I decided to talk with him about the problem, and if he decided not to change, I would get out of the relationship.

The next time Steve got angry and started yelling at me, I told him in a polite way to not shout at me. Then we talked about possessiveness and jealousy. I tried listening to him so we could maybe solve this. Steve said he wanted to change, so we decided to try and work it out and keep going together.

The next time Steve saw me talking to another guy in my English class, he reacted the same as before: He got angry and started yelling at me. So I told him I didn't think I could be in a relationship with him and that I didn't want to go out with him anymore. Boy, was that a hard decision for me to make! I didn't want to hurt Steve, and I did have a good time with him when he wasn't angry. But I decided that fighting was not the kind of relationship I wanted with a boyfriend, so I chose to respond to Steve differently by not letting him get to me.

It's possible that both Jodi and Steve have mistaken beliefs that caused problems in their relationship. For example, Jodi may believe *I'm special only when I have a boyfriend* or *Jealousy is a sign of caring for someone.* Steve may believe *Men are supposed to be the boss in a relationship* or *I can use anger to control other people.* They formed these beliefs when they were very young, and their beliefs got in the way of what might have been a healthy relationship. Jodi has already decided to do things differently. She no longer believes that jealousy is a sign of caring and realizes she's worthwhile with or without a boyfriend.

You might want to think about your relationships—with parents, siblings, girlfriends, boyfriends. Which ones tend to have problems? Is it possible that you have some mistaken beliefs, and that these are causing conflict? Becoming aware of mistaken beliefs gives you the power to change them.

Changing Channels on Mistaken Beliefs

What happens when our expectations don't match reality? More conflict! Often, our expectations are based on mistaken beliefs. For example, if you formed the belief when you were young that *I should be able to do what I want, when I want to do it,* then you expect this to always be true for you. When it isn't, you feel frustrated and angry.

If you can use your imaginary remote control to change your thoughts and feelings, you can also use it to change your mistaken beliefs. In reality, no one can always do what they want, when they want to do it. Life simply doesn't work that way. When you feel yourself getting frustrated and angry, change the channel away from your mistaken belief to something more realistic and empowering. Instead of *I should be able to do what I want, when I want to do it,* you might think, *I don't necessarily like what's going on right now, but I know I can get through this,* or *I know I can't always get my way, and this happens to be one of those times.* Your frustration and anger will change to hope and confidence in your abilities to deal with the situation at hand.

The Problem with Reverse Control

How often have you done the opposite of what someone told you to do, just to prove that you could, even though it's not in your own best interests? This is called *reverse control,* and it's a common response to conflict.

For example: Your father expects you to maintain a B average in school. He reminds you often, and you don't like being told what to do. In fact, you're sick of hearing about it. You decide to prove to your father that he can't *make* you do anything. You stop doing your homework and start skipping classes. Your grades plummet from B's to D's and F's.

You certainly showed your dad a thing or two . . . but at what cost? You hurt him, but you hurt yourself more. Now it looks as if you'll have to repeat some of your classes, go to summer school (which means that you can't return to the job you enjoyed last summer), and possibly transfer to a new school next fall, away from your friends.

When you do the opposite of what your father wants you to do, you're *reacting,* not acting. You're basing your choices on his expectations, not on what's best for you. You're still allowing him to control you.

When you feel yourself giving in to reverse control, stop and ask yourself, "Is this what I really want? What will the consequences of my choices be?"

SUE ANNE: I Can't Believe I Quit Doing Something I Loved Just to Prove That I Can't Be Controlled

I love to dance. I've been dancing since I was in about the second grade—ballet, tap, jazz, toe, and dance line. For a while, I was dancing four nights a week, and I never got tired of it! My parents expect me to participate in some type of after-school activity, and dance was perfect.

When I was 13, I started hanging out with some kids who did nothing after school *except* hang out. My parents were on my back about staying in dance and not being a bum like my friends. They nagged me so much that I decided to quit dance line so I could be with my friends one more night a week. But what my parents said was, "If you aren't dancing, then you're staying home and doing homework!" We argued a lot, and, of course, I didn't stay home—no way. I started lying about where I was and what I was doing.

Before too long, I quit tap and started smoking. Then I quit toe and fought even more with my parents. Eventually, I quit dance completely, smoked a pack and a half a day, and drank on weekends—all to show my parents they could NOT control me and tell me what to do!

And here I am at 17, trying to quit smoking (I'm down to a half-pack of lights a day), out of shape, and about 25 pounds heavier than I want to be. A couple of friends and I were talking the other night about how, four years ago, we never dreamed we would be like this today. I mentioned how much I miss dance, and one of my friends said, "So, why don't you start dancing again?"

I've enrolled in a jazz class this fall, and I hope to not be smoking at all by then. I know it'll be really hard, but I can't wait! I can't believe I quit doing something I loved just to prove that I can't be controlled. I hurt my dad (which was what I wanted to do back then), but the person I hurt most was myself. I can't wait to get back into the one thing I love. It's not too late.

Cutting the Strings

Picture yourself as a puppet, with strings attached to your arms and legs. From the time you're born, your parents pull the strings. At some point during adolescence, teens usually decide that it's time for a change. When your parents pull your strings, you pull back.

Like reverse control, this is *reaction*, not action. You're still letting your parents determine what you will do—be pulled, or pull back in response to their pulling. What you can learn to do is cut the strings. *You can decide what you want to do.* Your options include:

1. doing what your parents ask or expect of you,
2. not doing what your parents ask or expect of you, or
3. negotiating another choice with them.

If you choose #3, you can use the speaking and listening skills described in Chapter 8, pages 126–135, to explain your point of view, hear theirs, and arrive at a compromise. Either way, you're acting, and not just reacting.

Self-Ideal vs. Self-Concept

Another potential cause of conflict has to do with your *self-ideal* (the way you think you *should be*) and your *self-concept* (the way you *really* are).

MARY: I Think I'm Overweight; I'd Like to Be Taller and Thinner

I'm 14 years old and an eighth grader. My father is 5'8" and weighs about 190 pounds. Mom is 5'4" and weighs about 140 pounds. Right now I'm very active in sports, and I'm what I would call "solidly built"— I'm 5'5" and weigh 135 pounds. I diet and I run every day, even after softball practice. I think I'm overweight; I'd like to be taller and thinner.

I know my family is concerned about me, because they say I don't have the body frame to weigh much less than my present weight. My mom and dad nag me constantly to eat more and exercise less. Life at my house isn't pleasant for anyone right now because of all the yelling and arguing about my weight.

Mary's self-ideal is that she should be tall and thin, but her self-concept (what she sees in the mirror) is that she's short and stocky. This is causing problems for her and her relationship with her parents.

The farther apart your self-ideal and self-concept are, the bigger your problems are likely to be. Becoming aware of this gives you the power to bring your two "selves" closer together. You can change your self-ideal, change your self-concept, or change both, depending on what works best for you.

Sometimes the reality of the situation makes it difficult or impossible to change one or the other. Mary will probably have more success if she works on changing her self-ideal. She wants to be taller and thinner, but both of her parents are short and stocky, and it's not likely that she will ever be 5'9" and weigh 120 pounds—it's just not in her genes. Mary can choose to accept her body the way it is and maintain her health through a sensible diet and moderate exercise. If that's what she decides to do, she will significantly reduce her inner conflict and her conflict with her parents.

Here's another example: Imagine that your self-ideal is that you should be physically fit. However, you know that you don't get enough exercise—plus you smoke at least a pack of cigarettes every day—so your self-concept is that you're in poor physical shape. This results in inner conflict.

You can change your self-ideal to "I should work on taking care of myself." And you can change your self-concept by taking better care of yourself. You might sign up for a stop-smoking program, ask your doctor to help you quit smoking, cut down on the number of cigarettes you smoke each day, and/or start an exercise program. Anything you do to bring your self-concept closer to your self-ideal will lessen the inner conflict you feel.

Nine Steps to Solving Problems

What can you do when a problem you're having with another person gets out of hand? Don't give up. You can still bring yourself (and the situation) back under control.

First, *cool down*. Here are some ideas you can try:

- Count to ten before saying anything further.
- Take deep breaths.
- Leave the room.
- Become aware of what you're thinking and feeling. Remember who's in control of your thoughts and actions.
- Take a walk.

Once you're feeling calmer, come back to discuss the problem. Then try this step-by-step strategy:

1. *Listen* carefully so you can determine what the real problem is. Use reflective listening and active listening (see pages 132–135). Use "I messages" (see pages 128–132) to express your point of view.
2. *Think* of all possible solutions without judging the merit of any of them. You might want to write down your ideas so you don't forget any in the process of deciding which one to try.
3. *Discuss* solutions and eliminate any that aren't okay with both of you.
4. *Look* at the consequences of each remaining solution.
5. *Choose* a solution.
6. *Agree* to the solution, either verbally or in writing.
7. *Set a time* to meet again and decide if the solution is working. Depending on the problem you're trying to

solve, you might meet again in a week, a month, or at the end of the school quarter.

8. *Act* on the solution. Try it out.

9. *Evaluate* the solution. Take time to sit down with the other person and talk about it. If the solution is working, congratulate yourself (and each other). If the solution isn't working, remember that everyone makes mistakes. Then consider these questions:

- What happened?
- Why didn't it work?
- What do I/we need to do differently?

Afterward, agree to try another solution. It's not the end of the world; it's simply time to choose something else.

KIM: The More the Teacher Tried to Get Me to Settle Down, the More I Acted Up

I'm 13 and in seventh grade. Normally I'm a pretty good student, receiving B's and C's. This year, I was in choir because I love to sing. I'd really like to have a career in music someday. But about the middle of the first trimester, I started having a problem with my choir teacher.

I like having a good time, and I do some talking in class, so my choir teacher came down hard on me. I was sent to detention a couple of times and got discipline slips. The more the teacher tried to get me to settle down, the more I acted up. I actually ended up failing choir in that power struggle with my teacher.

Well, my first reaction to the problem was to drop choir and quit the program. But I talked with the school social worker, who tried to show me other choices besides giving in to the teacher or quitting choir. She first had me figure out what the real problem was: I didn't want to allow the choir teacher to control me, and I think there was some kind of a personality conflict.

The social worker sat down with me, and together we listed all of the possible solutions to the problem. This was my list:

—quit choir
—yell at the teacher
—write a nasty letter to the teacher
—talk to the teacher
—have a conference with the teacher, my parents, and me
—meet with the teacher, social worker, and me
—report the teacher to the principal
—continue to cause problems in class and fail choir again.

A long list!

I talked these solutions over with the social worker, and we eliminated some ideas right away that just weren't okay with me. Then we figured out how each of the other solutions would turn out. I decided to try talking to the teacher with the social worker present.

The meeting took place, and both the choir teacher and I were able to lay out our sides of the problem. We agreed on behavior we were both okay with and decided that I didn't have to quit choir. We also agreed that the three of us would meet again a month later to check in. I'm glad I didn't decide to quit choir.

10

Building Better Relationships

Relating well to others involves talking, listening, and knowing how to sort out problems and handle conflicts. If you haven't yet read chapters 8 and 9, you might want to read them now. The stronger your skills in these areas are, the stronger and healthier your relationships will be, and the less likely you'll be to turn to alcohol, drugs, nicotine, and food to smooth out the bumps in life.

Deciding What's Important in Your Relationships

If someone asked you to list the qualities of a good relationship, what would you say? Take a minute to think about this. Then, if you want, write your list on a separate sheet of paper.

Here are ten things teens often say are important to them in their relationships:

1. Respect.
2. Trust.
3. Having the space to be myself and to grow.
4. Fun.
5. A sense of humor.

"I would like to be someone who is trustworthy, honest, and caring."
Althea, 15

6. Similar likes and interests.

7. People who accept me for who I am, without wanting me to change.

8. Honesty.

9. Caring.

10. Kindness.

"I would like to be someone who's brave and who stands up for what they believe (which I do, but I would like to do it more) and for people to look up to me as someone special."

Bonnie, 15

You can learn a lot about your relationships by "rating" them for each of these qualities. On the next page is a checklist you can use to do this. (Or you can create your own checklist from your own list of qualities.)

Choosing Healthy Relationships

If a relationship doesn't meet your standards, you can do something about it. Start by assessing your own self-esteem. Do you believe that you deserve to be treated with respect, trust, honesty, caring, and kindness? If not, you may be seeking out relationships with people who treat you badly. Do you accept yourself for who you are? If not, you may be looking for someone to control you and change you.

Walk Away from Abuse

What if you're in a relationship with someone who hits you or pushes you around? Who puts you down with words or calls you names? Who demands that you do sexual things you don't want to do? Who gives you the silent treatment or plays guilt games with you? Call the abuse by its name and walk away.

Rating Relationships: A Checklist

Think of a relationship that's important to you. Read through the qualities listed here, then rate your relationship according to each quality. Use a scale of 0–10, with 0 meaning "this relationship doesn't have this quality at all" and 10 meaning "this relationship has this quality 100 percent of the time."

rating   characteristic

———— 1. Respect.

———— 2. Trust.

———— 3. Having the space to be myself and to grow.

———— 4. Fun.

———— 5. A sense of humor.

———— 6. Similar likes and interests.

———— 7. People who accept me for who I am, without wanting me to change.

———— 8. Honesty.

———— 9. Caring.

———— 10. Kindness.

This exercise can give you a clear idea of how that person fits your definition of a good relationship. Don't expect any relationship to be a perfect 10 in all areas. Ratings in the range of 6 and above indicate relationships that are on the healthy side.

Here's how you can call abuse by its name:

- Hitting, pushing, and other actions that hurt your body are *physical abuse*.
- Put-downs and name-calling are *verbal abuse*.
- Demands to do sexual things you don't want to do are *sexual abuse*.
- The silent treatment and guilt games are *emotional abuse*.

How can you tell if you're being abused? You don't feel good about what's happening, and you make excuses for the other person's behavior—to other people and to yourself. Such as:

- "He/she didn't really mean it."
- "He/she won't do it again."
- "If I hadn't done that/acted like that, he/she wouldn't have treated me that way."
- "I asked for it."
- "I really deserved that."

In fact, the other person is responsible for his or her words and actions—just as you are responsible for yours. If abuse happens once, it's likely to happen again. Abuse is never your fault, and you *never* "deserve it."

People who resort to abuse probably learned to handle their problems in this way when they were very young. They are operating out of mistaken beliefs. Don't wait around to find out why or to "help" them. Don't try to change them, because you can't. Walk away from the abuse as fast as you can. If you need help, talk to an adult you trust. For suggestions on finding a safe adult, see pages 182–185.

Get the Space You Need

You've just met the "perfect person." Sparks fly, the chemistry is powerful, you can't believe how many interests you share, and the two of you become inseparable—dating happily, getting serious, enjoying each other immensely. You feel as if you've finally found the relationship that's going to last forever. Then one of you announces, "I feel like I'm being smothered; I need to back off for a while. I need my own space!"

This causes pain for both of you, but it reveals an important truth: Even in seemingly "perfect" relation-

"In any relation-ship, you share your personality. That's non-negotiable. But your body belongs to you. You have a choice about whether you want to share that with some-one else. Always remember that you have the right to say no."
Lynda, 15

ships, both people need space—physical, mental, and emotional—in which to grow.

In a healthy relationship, each person has the space to "do their own thing." You have fun together and still spend time apart from each other. You have friends in common and friends who are yours alone. You feel free to pursue interests that the other person doesn't share; you have your own opinions, even if they differ from the other person's. You respect each other as unique individuals, with unique dreams and goals. You want what's best for each other.

Do Your Part

If you completed the "Rating Relationships" checklist on page 151, look back at it again. Rate yourself for each quality from 1–10. Are you doing *your* part to make sure that your relationship is one of mutual respect, trust, honesty, caring, kindness, and acceptance?

Healthy relationships take work. Both people need to do their part, to give and take, to compromise or change if necessary. Neither person in a relationship is more important than the other; neither should be more powerful. When problems arise, you should both be able to talk about them, express your feelings, and reach an agreement together about what to do. Try the speaking and listening skills described on pages 128–135; use the problem-solving strategy outlined on pages 146–147.

A Relationships Continuum

All relationships are not the same. Throughout your lifetime, you'll have various types of relationships. You might picture them as falling along a continuum, like this:

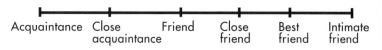

Acquaintance   Close   Friend   Close   Best   Intimate
                acquaintance   friend   friend   friend

What are the differences among the various types of relationships? Here are some definitions to consider:

- *Acquaintance:* Someone whose face looks familiar; a person you've seen before but you don't know well enough to hold a conversation with. This might be someone you see in a class or the hall, someone you smile at and greet but don't speak to.

- *Close acquaintance:* Someone you know well enough to speak to on occasion. This person might be in a few of your classes; you might discuss homework or the teacher with this person, but you wouldn't call the person or hang out with him or her.

- *Friend:* Someone you sit next to in class, walk with in the halls, eat lunch with, or call outside of school to talk or visit. You trust this person enough to share some private feelings and thoughts.

- *Close friend:* Someone you spend a lot of time with, making weekend plans and perhaps spending the night at each other's homes. You might share more personal information with this person.

- *Best friend:* The person you choose to spend a lot of time with. You feel a sense of camaraderie and share special feelings. You can tell a best friend almost anything. (It's possible to have more than one best friend.)

- *Intimate friend:* The person you can tell anything to and trust it will go no further. You can be completely yourself without being judged or put down. *Important:* We aren't talking sexual intimacy here. We're talking *emotional* intimacy. This is a special relationship!

Each of us is constantly moving in and out of relationships along this continuum. Even a best friend or an intimate friend starts out as an acquaintance. You meet someone, decide you'd like to know the person better, and decide to do something together; you enjoy each other's company, trust grows, and over a period of time you become closer. Your relationship moves along the continuum from left to right.

Some relationships move along the continuum from right to left. People change, interests change, schedules conflict, or other things happen and you don't spend as much time together as you used to. You learn that you can trust certain people more than others, and that defines the type of relationship you share.

To learn more about your relationships, you might want to think of one person in your life who fits each description on the continuum. Then go back to the checklist on page 151 and rate those relationships. It makes sense to expect that the relationships at the right of the continuum will have more of the qualities named in the checklist. If they don't, you may want to reexamine your relationships and what they mean to you.

11

Forming More Positive Beliefs and Behaviors

Building a strong relationship with *yourself* is an important and often neglected part of growing up. Girls in particular are often taught to take care of others first. Being aware of the needs of others is important, but balancing your needs with what others ask of you is also important.

Understanding your own behavior is a good place to start. Why do you do the things you do? If you can answer that question, you'll be light-years ahead of many people in terms of your capacity to have healthy, respectful relationships—with yourself and others. This chapter will give you some insights into how you approach life.

"I like who I am, and I'm glad that I don't wish I was like anyone else. I might envy others for certain things, but I'd only like to be me."
Clare, 15

MELISSA: I Was Positive That No One Liked Me

When I was in sixth grade, I had *no* friends. None! When we had to choose partners for science class, I broke out in a sweat because I was afraid I would end up with the kid who never showered. I usually ended up alone or with some other poor soul who was also sweating because no one would match up with them. Lunch was the worst. I roamed the cafeteria looking for an empty seat next to someone who wouldn't make some rude remark about my being there.

Every school day seemed endless, and every morning I got sick when the alarm went off. Because I was positive that no one liked me, I would sit and read a book instead of trying to talk with others. It was safer. If someone did talk to me, it was usually an insult or sarcastic joke, and I would pout or escape to the bathroom and cry.

In seventh grade, things got even worse. Once I invited seven girls to a Spring Break party at my house, and only one showed up. I tried some after-school activities, but it was too hard for me to talk to the other kids, and I usually ended up sitting alone. My parents kept telling me to have friends over, and they didn't seem to understand that no one *wanted* to come over.

By the middle of seventh grade, I was spending a lot of time in the counselor's office at school. I had started fighting with girls in my class. I suppose I was fed up and had decided to get back at everyone for the way I was feeling. The counselor helped me to see why I was so angry (from years of being put down and being made fun of). I figured out some things I was doing that made my classmates feel uncomfortable around me. I realized I wasn't joining in. I was being sarcastic because I was afraid of being rejected, and I was trying to get their attention. The counselor and I also discussed what I could do differently in order to be accepted. She helped me to understand myself better and why I chose to act the way I did.

By ninth grade, I was in a new school, ready to start over and try some new ways of making friends. By the middle of ninth grade, things were better. I understood myself better, and I knew more about how to get along with others. I wish I could say that I'm now in the "popular" group, but I can't. I do have a few friends I can hang out with, and we have a good time. My meetings with the counselor helped a lot. I'm glad I found her.

How Mistaken Goals Can Affect Behavior

Why do we sometimes do things that hurt us? Why do we act in ways that alienate others, get us in trouble, and make us unhappy? Psychiatrist Alfred Adler believed that all behavior has a purpose, even if that purpose isn't always clear, doesn't always make sense, and often lies below the surface of our conscious awareness. When we can figure out the purpose behind an action, we can decide what to do about it. Knowledge gives us the power to change.

We've learned a lot about behavior and its causes from another psychiatrist, Rudolph Dreikurs, who studied with Alfred Adler and worked closely with families and children. As Dreikurs observed children, he noticed that their misbehavior seemed to have four main causes. He called these *mistaken goals*—"goals" because even though they got the children in trouble, they also achieved something the children wanted. These goals are often related to mistaken beliefs.

Dreikurs' four mistaken goals are:

1. attention,
2. power,
3. revenge, and
4. feeling inadequate.

As you read the following sections and stories, see if any of these mistaken goals sound familiar to you.

Mistaken Goal #1: Attention

Do your friends, parents, and other people you know seem annoyed by some of the things you do? Do they ever say, "Stop that!" or "Cut it out!" and roll their eyes or shake their heads? Do you do things on purpose that you know might get you into trouble? Are you the class clown? A show-off? A pest? Do you procrastinate, whine, and make sarcastic remarks? If so, you might be seeking attention in inappropriate ways.

You might be guided by mistaken beliefs, such as *I only count when I'm the center of attention,* or *I only count when people pay attention to me,* or *Any kind of attention is better than being ignored or not being noticed.* Attention can be either positive or negative. If you're attracting negative attention, how can you turn that around into

positive attention? Consider your strengths and assets—your special skills. Figure out how you can share them with others. Be cooperative, respectful, and encouraging to others. You might attract so much positive attention that you won't need any more negative attention.

MONICA: I Have to Admit, I Liked the Splash I Made

I used to sneak into classrooms each morning before school and write swear words and other graffiti on blackboards. Although no one in the administration knew who was doing it, some of my friends did. And I told a counselor I was seeing outside of school.

One day, the counselor asked me, "Monica, why are you doing this? What do you get out of it? What's the pay-off?" I had to admit, I liked the splash I made and all the attention my words were getting. The counselor helped me to realize that this kind of attention was negative and uncool. Together we came up with better ways for me to get attention.

I'm really good at writing poetry, so I started writing for the school newspaper. When my writing was published, I found that I got the attention I wanted from my friends and other kids in the school, without running the risk of getting caught writing trash on blackboards.

Mistaken Goal #2: Power

Do you get into power struggles with your parents, teachers, and other people you know? Are you sometimes (or often) bossy, defiant, stubborn, belligerent, manipulative, and/or super-competitive? Do adults ever tell you that you have an attitude? If so, you might be seeking power in inappropriate ways.

If you have frequent power struggles, you might be guided by mistaken beliefs, such as *I only count when I get my way,* or *I only count when I'm in control,* or *I have to win all the time at everything I do.* In power struggles, there are no winners. At some point, everyone ends up feeling frustrated, angry, and sad. Even the person who seems to get his or her way isn't really a winner.

How can you put a stop to power struggles? First, you can choose not to start or take part in arguments. If an argument seems unavoidable, try to remove yourself from the situation. Leave the room, take a walk, and cool down. If you can't leave, take deep breaths or count to ten. When you're feeling more calm, less reactive, and more in control of your thoughts and feelings, try using the speaking and listening techniques described on pages 128–135. Don't get involved in power struggles, and you'll discover how powerful you really are.

GINGER: I Wish There Was a Better Way to Solve Problems Around My House

I'm 15 and a freshman in high school. I constantly fight with my parents, and sometimes I can't stand them. They never seem to respect me or my opinions.

One day not too long ago, they told me I could go to a party at a friend's house on Saturday and spend the night. The day before the party, they told me I couldn't go because the school counselor had called them and said I'd been caught smoking in between classes.

I got so angry at them for changing their minds that I started yelling at them. "You don't respect me at all!" I screamed. They yelled back that I didn't respect them. I screamed even louder and started calling them names. They ordered me to go to my room. Instead, I ran out the door and went to another friend's house to cool off. When I came back home a few hours later, the doors were all locked and no one answered. I just kept banging on the door until they finally let me in.

That was one of the worst nights of my life. We argued for what seemed like hours until I finally ran to my room and slammed the door. Now I'm grounded for at least a month, so I guess they won. I wish there was a better way to solve problems around my house.

Mistaken Goal #3: Revenge

Do you try to get back at people you feel have treated you badly or unfairly? Do you wish you could hurt them as much as they hurt you? Acts of revenge can range from talking back, to crimes such as shoplifting, stealing, or vandalism. Some teens use drinking, drugs, and smoking as ways to get back at their parents. Others deliberately reject the values important to their parents by skipping classes, refusing to attend religious services, or becoming sexually active.

FELICIA: More Than Anything, I Wanted to Get Back at My Father

I tried to beat the mail home each day because I knew an envelope from school would be arriving. I'd been skipping science and math classes because I was behind, and I knew I was failing. One day when I got home, I knew I'd missed the mail by the look on my father's face. Good grades and getting an education are very important to my father.

He was so angry and hurt that he grounded me for the rest of the quarter (about two months) with no discussion! I was angry and hurt, too—both because of the way he overreacted, and because being with my friends is extremely important to me. More than anything, I wanted to get back at him. I even thought about running away. That would prove he couldn't control me, and it would drive him crazy with worry. I haven't done it yet, but maybe next time I will. I just wish he'd talk to me, instead of punishing me.

If you act out of revenge, you may be guided by mistaken beliefs, such as *I only count when I'm hurting you the way you've hurt me,* or *Anyone who hurts me deserves to be hurt back.* Revenge is a dangerous game, and it stops only when one of you decides not to play anymore. If you genuinely feel that a parent is being unfair, try talking instead of retaliating. Share your feelings and work together on coming up with solutions. Use "I messages," reflective listening, and active listening (see pages 128–135). Try a problem-solving strategy (see pages 146–147). Do whatever you can to break the cycle of revenge.

Mistaken Goal #4: Feeling Inadequate

It's hard to picture "feeling inadequate" as a goal, but sometimes it is. The mistaken beliefs that guide this goal might go something like this: *I only count when I convince others that I'm helpless,* or *People shouldn't expect anything of me,* or *It's no use trying.* People who are seeking this goal may show it by these kinds of behaviors:

- not taking care of themselves physically (using alcohol, drugs, or tobacco; not eating properly; not bathing; not caring about how they look),
- not showing up for class or school,
- acting helpless ("I can't do this! I don't understand this! I can't handle this!"),
- having a hard time getting out of bed,
- not being interested in activities they used to enjoy,
- acting sad, numbed, or depressed, and/or
- refusing to do or try anything that takes effort.

If you see yourself anywhere in this list, get help. Talk to a school social worker, a counselor, a therapist, or someone else who can help you understand why you are feeling so inadequate—and how you can start feeling and acting like the strong, capable person you really are.

Two More Mistaken Goals

Besides attention, power, revenge, and feeling inadequate, there are two more mistaken goals that can cause problems in your life: seeking excitement and responding to peer pressure in ways that are potentially harmful for you.

Seeking Excitement

Excitement is usually associated with risk taking or danger. Self-destructive ways of seeking excitement include using alcohol and other drugs, drinking and driving, playing "chicken" in cars, drinking games, shoplifting, vandalism, "tagging" (writing graffiti), and being sexually active before you're ready. The mistaken belief that guides these choices might go something like this: *I can experience real excitement only if I put myself in danger.*

There are other ways to get an adrenaline "rush" without risking long-term negative consequences. For example, you might choose to play in a band, get involved in theater or debate, ride a roller coaster, or take up a challenging physical activity such as downhill skiing, diving, parachuting, parasailing, rock climbing, running, riding dirt bikes, in-line skating, skateboarding, or competitive sports.

"I would like to be well-educated, with a lot of different skills. I want to live life to the fullest, raise a family, relax, enjoy life, and go to the moon."
Cho, 14

> **KALI: Who Needs Drugs to Get High?**
>
> I play trumpet in the school band and in the jazz band. I don't do drugs or drink, and I don't smoke. I

165

don't do sex. I'm often referred to as the "band nerd," but that's okay. There was a time when that really bothered me. But I really enjoy playing the trumpet, and I decided not to let other people take that away from me.

At the end of my junior year, two professional trumpet players came to play at our school jazz concert. We got to play with them. During our last song, the two players came up on the risers and stood right next to me and played along with us. They didn't even need music. For me, it was the most awesome experience ever—the biggest adrenaline rush I'd ever had. Who needs drugs to get high?

Responding to Peer Pressure

A sense of belonging is something every person seeks. The need is good; it's what you do to meet it that can sometimes cause problems. Especially when you're guided by the mistaken belief that says, *I only count when I'm like everyone else*—even if "everyone else" is doing risky or dangerous things. Many teens choose to start using alcohol, drugs, and tobacco because "everyone else" is doing it, and the peer pressure is hard to resist.

There are many healthy ways to belong and to be valued. Join a club, go out for a sport, volunteer at a nursing home, or work with small children or kids with disabilities. Helping others is guaranteed to make you feel "connected."

If you're ever in doubt about a choice you're about to make (or have just made), ask yourself, "Why am I doing this?" or "Why did I do that?" Once you know the "why," you can take the next step: changing your behavior. Sometimes just figuring out the "why" can bring about instant change.

Justine: Good Friends Respect Your Beliefs and Choices

At the end of my sophomore year, I played soccer on a club team with other kids from all over the city. I convinced my parents to let me spend the day with two of my soccer friends who lived about 40 miles from my house.

At first, we had a blast. We joined up with two more friends of theirs and went out to eat. Three of the girls got up and left after lunch. I thought they were in the next room, but they were gone for a long time. When I went to check, they were in their car smoking weed.

My soccer friends knew I didn't use drugs. I had decided not to drink or use drugs for lots of reasons, one being sports—I want to be the best women's soccer player in the country. There was no way I was getting in the car with those kids who, by now, were high.

I tried calling my parents, but there was no answer. I was so upset—40 miles from home with no ride. I finally called a school friend who was old enough to drive, and she agreed to come pick me up.

I know now that my soccer friends are not what I call good friends. Good friends don't put you in a position of doing things you don't believe in. Good friends respect your beliefs and choices, even if those choices differ from theirs.

Controlling Your Dives and Climbs

Another approach to understanding your behavior and making positive changes is to think of the steps we typically follow from thought to action. Psychologist Albert Ellis described these steps in a way that's easy to understand:

"I'd like to be a country girl with a horse and house and vast land, a place I could call my own and where I would be me."
Sheryl, 17

167

1. First we have a *thought.*
2. That thought triggers a *feeling.*
3. That feeling gives us the energy to *act.*
4. Our actions produce more *thoughts.*

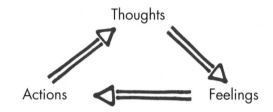

Imagine this cycle and picture yourself as a pilot flying a plane. This plane represents your feelings. While you're at the controls, you can dive or you can climb, depending on your thoughts. If your thoughts are negative, you'll feel bad and start a dive. If your thoughts are positive, you'll feel better and go into a climb. It's that simple.

Taking a Dive

A dive goes something like this: You have a negative thought—one of those countless silent messages we give ourselves, such as *This is stupid. I can't deal with this anymore.* This thought triggers feelings like anger, rage, frustration, hopelessness, and powerlessness.

When you're experiencing these feelings, you might choose to act by throwing things, yelling, arguing, crying uncontrollably, running away, shutting down, or doing nothing. If you react in these ways, you have more negative thoughts about yourself because you aren't solving the problem at hand.

Now you're in a dive. When you hit the lowest part of the dive, you crash into depression.

"This is stupid." (Thought)

⇓

Frustration, anger (Feelings)

⇓

Arguing, running away (Actions)

⇓

"I can't deal with this anymore." (Thought)

⇓

Hopelessness (Feeling)

⇓

Quitting, shutting down (Actions)

⇓

CRASH (Depression)

Going for a Climb

If you take a dive, it's up to you to pull out of it. You're at the controls of your plane. Sometimes you might have someone along (a copilot) who can help you—a parent, counselor, social worker, therapist, or other adult.

To pull out of the dive, you can change your thoughts, feelings, or actions. Changing your feelings is close to impossible. (If you could just feel better, you would!) Changing your actions is possible but very difficult. The way to start climbing out of a dive is by changing your thoughts.

Because thoughts trigger feelings, changing your thoughts can also change your feelings. First, become aware of some of those countless silent messages you give yourself, such as *This is stupid. I can't deal with this.* Change that negative message to a positive.

There's a trick to this, however. If you changed the message to *Life is wonderful and everything is great,* would you believe it? Probably not. At this moment, your life is not wonderful and things are not great. So the trick is to change the negative message to one that's both positive and believable, such as *This stinks. I don't like what's going on, but I know I can deal with it.* With this thought, you've started to pull out of your dive.

Positive, believable thoughts can produce feelings like hope, power, and confidence. Such feelings can give you the energy to talk about your problem, brainstorm solutions, get out of bed, confront someone, or do whatever is needed to solve the problem. You are now going for a climb.

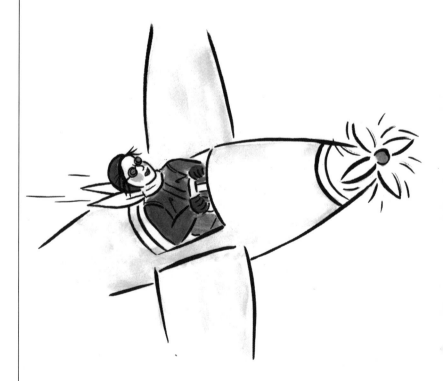

Self-confidence (Feeling)

⇑

"I did it." (Thought)

⇑

Talking and brainstorming (Actions)

⇑

Hope and power (Feelings)

⇑

"I know I can deal with it." (Thought)

Pulling out of a dive isn't easy. To avoid a crash, you need to learn skills that will help you start to climb. The only person who can do this is the person at the controls—you!

SHELLY: I Was So Fried That I Couldn't Remember Anything

I go to an alternative learning center instead of regular school because I flunked out. I'm 18 and have about a year and a half of full-time studying ahead of me before I can graduate. I have a supportive, caring family. My mom and dad work hard at their jobs and at parenting.

During my sophomore year of high school, I started hanging around with a new friend named Sara. I actually got to know her and felt sorry for her because both of her parents are alcoholics. I guess I thought I could help her. I tried to introduce her to my old group of friends (who could have a great time without chemicals), but she really didn't like them (and they didn't like her).

Because I felt sorry for Sara, I ended up dropping my old friends. It happened gradually; I wasn't really aware of what was happening. I eventually stopped hanging out with my old group altogether and instead started hanging out with Sara's friends. I felt so cool because we would sit around on weekends smoking pot and drinking beer. I really thought I had matured beyond my old group and felt like I belonged to a much more "in" crowd.

In order to feel accepted, I began smoking pot every day after school and on weekends. My old friends would have nothing to do with me or Sara. My grades started to go down because I was too busy smoking pot to go to classes and do homework. I was so fried that I couldn't remember anything. I started to break rules at home and get into arguments with my parents and brother. At one point, my parents told me I would have to move out if I didn't enroll in school full-time and get a job.

Sara and I both arranged to attend the alternative program in our school district, where we felt we would fit in better. I continued smoking pot, only now I was smoking during lunch and breaks at school. I ended up on probation at school because I wasn't turning in any work and was missing classes again. I got more and more depressed, argued with my parents, and felt like I wasn't any good.

One day, my English teacher at the alternative school made a deal with me: He wouldn't drop me from school if I agreed to see the school counselor. I knew that if I got dropped, I would be kicked out of my house, so I agreed. I began meeting with the counselor and really thought it was stupid. I didn't understand why I had to go, and I started to resent having to see him (especially when he started telling me he was concerned about my pot use).

Things went from bad to worse. Fighting with my family became very regular, turning in work at school became very difficult, and I was more and more depressed. During one of my sessions with the counselor, he told me he thought I was depressed and would like me to think about seeing a psychiatrist. At first, I thought he was crazy, but after thinking about it for a while and doing an inventory of my life (arguing with my caring family, failing school when I once made good grades, losing good friends, being unable to get a job, and using pot more and more), I decided it might be a good idea. Besides, I didn't want to get kicked out of my house.

I presented the suggestion to my mom, who immediately called and made an appointment. I was about to be dropped from school, but I convinced my advisor that I was in the process of making changes in my life. I decided to quit using pot cold turkey. It was difficult, but I was convinced that pot was the reason for my depression and failing, so I hung in there.

I continued to hang out with Sara and her friends, but they were still using regularly. I started to see what a waste it was and how we were ruining our lives. I gradually began staying at home more and spending less time with the group. I began to get along with my folks and not argue as much. I became more cooperative at home and helped out with chores. I cleaned up my physical appearance and started applying for jobs. I also began turning in work at school.

I'm trying to hook up with my old group of friends, but they won't return my calls. I suppose they don't want to have anything to do with me. I have a great deal of proving to do to many people. As I think back on the last two years, I've been trying to figure out why I ever chose to use pot. The only thing I can come up with is this: It made me feel special, like I was cool and belonged with a popular group. I had always wanted to be popular, and being in this large group made me think I was. I didn't realize that no one really cared about me because they were all so busy getting high. It was a false feeling. I wish I'd never made those decisions in the first place. But I'm working on forgiving myself and moving on.

12

Taking Good Care of Yourself

Being Assertive

You have many needs—for belonging, friendship, respect, understanding, and the freedom to make decisions that affect your life. What's the best, most effective way to take care of yourself and get your needs met? First, consider two ways that DON'T work:

Be Passive. Don't speak up for yourself. Don't say what you really mean. When you do speak, use a soft, timid voice, look at the floor instead of at the person you're addressing, and apologize for bothering the person. Better yet, don't say anything and hope that the other person will read your mind.

Be Aggressive. Try to intimidate the other person with your actions and your words. Stand with your feet apart, hands on hips; speak in a loud voice, make demands and accusations, use "you messages," glare at the other person, point at the other person, and bully the other person. Take the offensive and don't back down.

When you're passive, it's easy for other people to ignore you and not take you seriously. When you're aggressive, others are too busy defending themselves to consider your needs. If you really want people to care about your needs and perhaps even help you to meet them, here's an approach that DOES work:

> *Be Assertive.* Stand or sit comfortably, make eye contact with the other person, and state your needs clearly in a firm, warm voice. Use "I messages" (see pages 128–132) and active listening (pages 134–135); say what you mean and mean what you say. Show by your body language, facial expressions, and tone of voice that you're strong, confident, and self-assured. Be respectful and expect respect in return.

When you're assertive, you can share your feelings without being embarrassed or ashamed. You can describe what you need and negotiate with others to get your needs satisfied. You can take care of yourself and say no when necessary. When you're assertive, you also have boundaries; you know what your limits are, and you know when they've been crossed. You maintain your boundaries by refusing to do things that aren't right for you, even if this means not going along with the group.

VICKI: I'm So Glad I Had the Courage to Stand Up for What I Believed

In seventh grade, I started hanging out with some kids I thought were having a lot of fun. They appeared to be happy and carefree, as if they knew how to have a great time. At first, we just hung out at each other's houses, but that got boring. So we moved on to the local café until we got kicked out for "loitering." We ended up wandering the streets, not doing anything in particular.

One evening, someone thought it would be fun to break into an expensive car and take the car stereo system. I was really scared. I knew what we were doing was wrong, and I knew if we got caught my parents would be very disappointed (and I would be in big trouble). So I mustered up all of my strength, pictured my father's face in my mind, and spoke up to my friends. I asked them if they thought they should really be doing this.

They were all caught up in the thrill of doing something illegal, and they made fun of me, calling me "chicken" (among other names). I can't believe how scared I was, both of being caught and of standing up to them and possibly losing their friendship. I finally decided to not get involved. All I could think of was the "guilt by association" lecture my parents had given me a couple of months earlier.

It was one of the hardest things I've ever done, but I told my friends that I wouldn't join them in taking something that wasn't mine. I left the group, found a pay phone at the café, and called my parents. Luckily, they were home. I was so afraid they would be angry at me when they picked me up. Instead, they told me how proud they were of the choice I had made.

I ended up losing those "fun" friends, but I decided they weren't doing the kinds of things I wanted to get involved in. If they really had been good friends, they would have respected my choice to not go along with them. Instead, they made fun of me whenever they saw me. I had a difficult couple of months after the "incident," but I called other kids and looked for new friends who were more like me. I have to admit I spent a few nights crying because I didn't think I had any friends. But with some effort on my part, that changed. The group never did get caught for that particular crime, but they have since been picked up for vandalism. I'm so glad I had the courage to stand up for what I believed!

Knowing Your Rights

Every person has basic human rights, but sometimes we forget our rights. Girls and women are especially prone to forgetting their rights. Knowing your rights and reviewing them often can support your efforts to be assertive.

You have the right to:

- Say no and voice your feelings.
- Say yes.
- Be heard, express your unique opinion, and make requests.
- Make mistakes without feeling guilty or ashamed.
- Like and respect yourself and be respected by others.
- Control your own life and set your own goals.
- Have privacy.
- Change your mind and make your own decisions.
- Love, laugh, be loved, and have fun.

"I see myself as a very strong, independent young adult."
Marcia, 17

Watching Out for Self-Fulfilling Prophecies

We all do it: We think or predict that something will happen, and it does. Or we say something that might not be true at the moment, but it later becomes true. Or we accept someone else's negative opinion of us and let it determine what we try to achieve.

If you keep telling yourself, "I'm no good," you'll keep putting yourself in a position to prove it. After all, you don't want to prove yourself wrong! Your negative thought becomes a *self-fulfilling prophecy.*

For example, Andrea believes that she's not very smart. People have told her for years not to expect too much of herself in school. So she doesn't do her homework, and she doesn't even try to succeed in school. As a result, her grades are very low. She has fulfilled the prophecy.

Self-fulfilling prophecies begin with those countless silent messages you give yourself throughout the day. In fact, Andrea doesn't lack intelligence; she just has problems in a particular subject. That doesn't make her stupid. It makes her like the rest of us—skilled in some areas and challenged in others.

Here's another example: Terry thought that her classmates didn't like her, so she acted in ways that alienated them. She was loud, annoying, pushy, and rude. Of course her classmates avoided her, which only proved to Terry that she'd been right all along.

Have you ever been caught in a self-fulfilling prophecy? Pay attention to the negative things you predict for yourself, or before you know it, they may come true. Take time to challenge the voice inside you that sometimes whispers, "I can't do it," or "I'm no good," or "Nobody likes me."

"I would like to be someone who doesn't worry what other people say and is always happy with the decisions I make. Always be yourself no matter what—that's the best."
Dana, 15

Avoiding Secrets

Secrets are interesting, and they can be fun. Two people in a special relationship will often share secrets. Girls send notes back and forth to best friends; teens form cliques and share secrets within the group. Knowing and keeping secrets makes us feel special or favored.

But secrets are also at the heart of many negative behaviors. Keeping secrets can lead to damaging isolation. Any time you feel like keeping a secret—from anyone—stop and ask yourself why. Are you trying to hide something? Is keeping this secret going to hurt someone? Is it going to hurt you?

Most self-destructive behaviors involve keeping secrets. We hide what we're doing, how much we're doing it, when, and with whom. Abusive relationships thrive on secrets. Abuse, whether it's physical, sexual, emotional, or verbal, happens and continues because someone keeps it a secret.

People who have struggled with addictions of any kind—to food, alcohol, drugs, or nicotine—will tell you that keeping secrets was part of their addictive behavior. You'll hear many stories of alcoholics who hid bottles all over the house, or drug addicts who hid their supplies, or people with eating problems who hid how much or how little they ate. Many of these stories come with other secrets that helped to conceal the self-destructive behaviors.

HEATHER: I Didn't Want Anybody to Know What He Was Really Like

I was a sophomore in high school when the biggest hunk of a senior started talking to me in the lunchroom. Greg was the captain of the football team, and everybody drooled over him. I couldn't believe he was talking to me! After a couple of weeks, he actually asked me out. I was so nervous I could hardly stand it. I couldn't eat, and of course had none of the right clothes to wear. We went to the school basketball game and out to eat afterwards. It was so cool—all the kids in the school saw me with him. I was in heaven.

We started going together, even though my parents weren't real excited about it because Greg was a senior. He was really nice, and my folks did like him, but they thought he was too old for me. I was on a high and *no one* was going to tell me I couldn't go out with Greg.

One night, Greg and I were at a party. Some kids had carried in alcohol, but I didn't care because I didn't drink. Greg seemed to respect my values and didn't try to force me to have a drink. To me, this made him even *more* perfect.

While we were at the party, I started talking to some other guys. Greg accused me of flirting, but I swear we were only having fun, and I was only talking. He became furious and started yelling at me and calling me names. I couldn't believe my ears. After the party broke up, we apologized and made up by making out. I was a little confused, because I had apologized for something I really didn't think I had done. But I had Greg back, and that was all that mattered.

As each week passed, Greg became more possessive of me, getting angry if I even looked like I was going to talk to another guy. He even got miffed if he called and I was on the phone with my girlfriends. I really couldn't understand this, but I still was going with the "hunk of the school," so I ignored my feelings of confusion, hurt, and fear. I wouldn't tell anybody because I didn't want to lose Greg, and I didn't want anybody to know what he was really like.

One day, when Greg was mad because I was late meeting him at his car after school, he shoved me into the parking lot fence. My arm hit the fencepost, and it left a huge bruise. I tried to wear long sleeves to hide it. My mom eventually saw the bruise, and of course she asked what happened. I told her I had run into the wall playing basketball in gym class.

During another argument with Greg, he became enraged and not only shoved me, but also punched me in the chest. I ended up with bruises again, and was able to hide them again. My relationship with Greg was getting pretty scary, but he was so nice and fun when he wasn't angry that I ignored the arguments. He became even more possessive, and each argument got more physical.

One day, a good friend of mine had me called to the school social worker's office to talk. My friend was concerned about my safety and about my relationship with Greg, so she had talked with the social worker. I started crying and told the social worker everything. I begged her to promise me she would tell no one, but after hearing about the arguments and abuse (only I wouldn't call it abuse), she said it was better to get it out into the open. She explained that keeping secrets was a way of allowing the abuse to continue happening. She asked me to keep on seeing her and talking about it.

I agreed to keep meeting with the social worker. As we continued talking, I began to see that I wasn't in a healthy relationship. My infatuation with Greg and the status I received at school had blinded me to what was really going on. I worked up enough courage to eventually break up with Greg, but it was incredibly hard. He was possessed with owning me and called me constantly.

When I look back on this experience, I wish I had done a few things differently. First, I wish I hadn't been in love with being in love with the most popular guy in school. Second, I wish I had left him the first time he shoved me. Third, I wish I had shared what was happening with a friend or adult. I needed to talk about my fears and concerns, I needed to be assertive with Greg, and I needed to stand up for myself.

I've had to work on forgiving myself for getting into that relationship and allowing myself to be harmed. But I also learned what I *will not* allow in future relationships. I wish I hadn't kept silent for so long, and I thank my friend for caring.

Secrets can be fine when you need a little privacy. But once in a while, take a look at the secrets you're keeping. Are they healthy secrets, or are they hurting you? Ask yourself why you're keeping the secrets, and question the motives of the person or people who want you to keep them. You may decide that keeping secrets isn't in your best interests. Share them with someone you trust. Sometimes taking good care of yourself means bringing secrets into the open.

Finding a Safe Adult

All girls (and boys) need at least one safe adult in their lives—someone who will act as a support person and, occasionally, an advocate. For many young people, a parent fulfills that role. But some teens can't rely on a parent, so they need to seek out another safe adult. That person can be almost anyone: a teacher, coach, neighbor, clergy member, aunt or uncle, youth leader, or friend's mother or father.

Safe adults are people who don't lecture you. Instead, they take time to listen and really hear you. They don't guess or assume that they know what's on your mind. They make eye contact with you when you're speaking. They accept you the way you are without trying to change you, and without making judgments. Instead of focusing on your weaknesses, they look for your strengths and talents.

Along with these wonderful qualities, safe adults:

- are honest, loyal, and "for real,"
- genuinely care about you,
- have boundaries for what they're willing to do for you,
- set limits on the behaviors they expect from you,
- may offer suggestions for what you can do, but only after listening and asking questions to help *you* decide what to do,
- are there when you need someone, or are willing to say, "I can't be there right now, but I can be there at this other time,"
- show respect for you as a person, and also for your feelings and beliefs, and
- share any concerns they might have as *concerns*, not as put-downs.

You might also seek out a mentor. Look around you for a woman you regard as a role model, someone you admire. She might be your mother, an adult relative, a teacher, a neighbor, or the mother of a friend. When you find your mentor, establish a bond. Seek her out to talk. Create opportunities to spend time together so you'll get a chance to observe more about who she is, how she relates to the world, how she handles conflicts and feelings, and how she conducts her relationships. Ask her questions about her life, about her growing-up years. As you get to know this person, and as she gets to know you better, you'll find that she's someone who can help you stay clear and sure. You'll also gain valuable information about living and relating in the world.

A safe adult will have the same qualities that define a healthy relationship (see the checklist on page 151). No one is perfect in all of these ways, but look for an adult who has most of these traits. If you look, you *will* find one!

LYNNE: I Never Knew It Was Possible to Have an Adult in My Life Who Would Be There for Me All the Time

After my parents divorced, my mom and I fought all the time. I was 13, and I smoked pot daily, skipped school, and got in enough trouble to end up in a foster home. That meant a new school, but I just found the same kinds of kids I used to know—the ones who used drugs—and I got in trouble all over again. My first foster family kicked me out for cheating, stealing, and lying to them. I ended up in another foster home.

I got really depressed and attempted suicide. Eventually, I ended right back at Mom's house. We did okay for a while, but we ended up going back to fighting. By this time, I was almost 15.

Then an interesting thing happened. A cousin in Boston said she'd take me in for a few months, so I flew out there. She and her husband sent me to a private school where the kids didn't drink, use drugs, or even smoke cigarettes. I started getting good grades.

My cousin and her husband set up very specific rules for me at home, encouraged me in anything I took an interest in, and even dragged me off to church every Sunday.

I got caught up in school and involved in church activities. I started working with younger kids. Not only did I stop using and drinking, but I also stopped smoking cigarettes because I didn't want to be a rotten role model for those kids.

The thing that made the difference for me, I think, were those two people—my cousin and her husband. They really cared about me and supported me and, I guess, believed in me. Before then, I never knew it was possible to have an adult in my life who would be there for me all the time. Now I have two!

Reducing Stress

Have you ever heard of *positive* stress? It exists. Positive stress is the kind that motivates you, helps you to achieve, and enables you to solve your problems.

We seldom hear about positive stress because the other kind gets most of the attention. Negative stress can lead to feelings of confusion, exhaustion, helplessness, sadness, fear, and depression. It can affect our bodies as well as our minds.

We all experience varying degrees of negative stress in our daily lives, and we all react differently. You may have heard some of your friends (and possibly your parents) say that they drink, use drugs, smoke, or eat to relieve stress. If you've read the first three parts of this book, you know that these "cures" don't work.

The next time you feel stressed out, try one or more of these stress-reducing techniques:

- If you're in a stressful situation, go somewhere else if at all possible.
- Do some deep breathing (in, hold, out, pause).
- Get some vigorous exercise. Take a brisk walk, go for a jog, ride a bike, go swimming, or do whatever it takes to boost your heart rate. Continue the activity for at least ten minutes.
- Do yoga.
- Meditate. Find a quiet, comfortable place to sit, then focus on . . . nothing. Try to empty your mind of all thoughts (and worries).
- Listen to calming music.

If you're having trouble sleeping at night, or if you need a dependable way to reduce your everyday stress level, use a relaxation technique. There are many books and audiocassettes that describe relaxation techniques; you may want to visit your local library and check some out. Meanwhile, you can try this technique, which uses the imaginary remote control first mentioned in Chapter 9 (see pages 136–138):

1. Find a quiet place where you can relax for several minutes without being interrupted or disturbed. Close your eyes.
2. Think of a positive experience from your life.
3. Push the button on your imaginary remote control and replay that positive experience. Relive the feelings that went along with the experience.Or, if you prefer, you can invent a visualization. Picture yourself in a calm and peaceful place. Think of the woods, canoeing on a river, sitting on a beach, or some other pleasant, comforting scene. "Record" your visualization in your mind.
4. Play back your positive experience or visualization whenever you need to relax.

Staying Clear and Sure

Throughout this book, we've tried to give you the information you need to take charge of your mind and body. We've spelled out the facts about alcohol, drugs, smoking, and eating problems, described some mistaken beliefs that can lead to trouble, shared first-person stories and quotes from girls who have "been there," and pointed toward places where you can find out more and get help. Because it's *your* mind and *your* body, what you do next is up to you.

We hope that you now have some tools you can use to make healthy choices about your life. We hope

"I want to be healthy, active, sociable. Successful (doing what I love, not for money), maybe a neurologist, maybe an actress, maybe a politician."
B.J., 15

187

that you'll choose to stay clear and sure. There will be times when it won't be easy—when life pressures, peer pressure, conflicts with friends and family members, mood swings, growing pains, and other stresses and strains will combine until you can hardly stand it. We want to leave you with a few more thoughts to help you through those difficult times.

Many recent studies have tried to determine why some kids make it through adolescence successfully while others don't. In fact, some young people who face big problems survive and thrive, while others who appear to have no problems stumble and fall as they move through their teens. The national survey done by PRIDE found that teens who have certain things going for them use drugs less than other teens. These clear, sure teens:

- participate in community activities,
- resist joining gangs,
- attend church or synagogue,
- find alcohol and other drugs hard to get,
- make good grades,
- take part in school activities,
- seldom have trouble at school,
- have parents who talk to them about drugs, and
- have parents who set and enforce clear rules about drug use.

The PRIDE Survey also found that drug use happens more often at home than in school, and it happens more often on weekends and when school isn't in session. In other words, there's a fairly simple way to strengthen your decision to avoid drinking and drugs: *Choose healthy, positive ways to spend your free time.*

MICKIE: What a Waste Those Years Were, When I Thought I Was So Cool

I guess you could say I've lived a lot of life in my 16 years. It's hard to believe that my past is really me.

When I think about it, I guess I would say it all started in sixth grade. Both of my parents worked and usually got home about 6:00 each evening or even later. Most of my friends in sixth grade were in some sort of after-school activity, like soccer, basketball, Odyssey of the Mind, or music lessons. That pretty much left me alone. Well, not really, because I started hanging out with some other kids who didn't do anything after school. At first, we just hung out at each other's empty houses. Then, for excitement and something different to do, we began stealing cigarettes from our parents, big sisters and brothers, and even from stores. We always smoked outside because we didn't want to smell up our houses and get caught.

Before long, cigarettes got boring, and we started smoking pot—at first only on weekends, then during the week, then once or twice a day—to get us through. Needless to say, my grades went down and I was arguing with my family a lot, but I still had my friends. After a while, even smoking pot got boring, and we started doing "shrooms" and acid on weekends.

One day, one of our buddies got caught with marijuana at school. The next thing you know, she had ratted on all of us and given the counselor and principal our names. Our parents were called in, and we had a conference. My parents aren't stupid. With all that had happened in the past year—my grades and all—they weren't about to believe my denials. So I went in for a urine test, and it was positive.

The next step was a treatment center for chemical abuse. It was absolutely horrible at first. No way was I going to cooperate—I wasn't a burnout like the other kids in that place (or so I thought). I ran away two or three times, thinking I would just go and live on my own at 15 and forget my family, especially my parents. At one point, I actually spent five days on the streets. It was cold, and I got very hungry.

Somehow the cops always found me and took me back to the center. One day, something clicked inside of me and I decided that if I really wanted to get out of that place, I'd better start cooperating. So I did.

You won't believe what happened . . . I learned to like myself. I learned to study again, budget my time, and develop some outside interests—like cross-age helping (when you help a younger kid by being a sort of big sister). I even started being a big sister to some of the kids who were new to the treatment center.

After 11 months, I graduated from the program and continued with an aftercare group. When it was time for me to attend school, I chose to go to a private school where I wouldn't be judged for my past. I was lucky my parents were willing and able to pay for me to do that.

At my new school, I'm still involved with a cross-age mentoring program after school, and I just love it. I've also been chosen as a peer counselor. (I think that all of the things I learned in treatment helped me to understand others better.) I've even started up a volunteer group to help homeless teens by collecting clothes and food for them.

My relationship with my parents is better, even though we still have some arguments. I think the big difference is that I'm active after school and I'm choosing to use my free time more wisely. I honestly don't have any desire to smoke, use pot, or drop acid anymore. I realize now how those things messed up my brain.

What a waste those years were, when I thought I was so cool! I'm glad now that my friend ratted on all of us. I hate to think where I would be today if she hadn't.

Resources

In researching and writing *Taking Charge of My Mind & Body*, we relied on our education, training, and expertise in each of our fields of experience, which include adolescent counseling and chemical use/abuse. We also consulted a number of experts, Web sites, and publications along the way. The Web sites are listed throughout the book and have been provided as additional resources for girls themselves. The sites will also be of interest and value to adults.

Many of the publications we depended on for our research can serve as resources for teachers, counselors, parents, and others who interact with and care about teenage girls. We found that valuable publications are available, often free of charge, from a number of national and local organizations like the ones listed below. (The addresses, phone numbers, and/or Web sites of these organizations have been provided throughout our book, and you can locate the organizations quickly by consulting our index.)

You can find out information about alcohol and other drug use from:

- the Center for Substance Abuse Treatment (CSAT),
- the National Clearinghouse for Alcohol and Drug Information (NCADI),
- the National Council on Alcoholism and Drug Dependence (NCADD),
- Alcoholics Anonymous,
- Cocaine Anonymous, and
- Al-Anon and/or Alateen.

You can order publications about the effects of smoking through:

- the American Cancer Society,
- the American Lung Association, and
- the American Heart Association.

Learn more about eating disorders from:

- the American Anorexia/Bulimia Association,
- Overeaters Anonymous, and
- the National Association of Anorexia Nervosa and Associated Disorders (ANAD).

Other resources we consulted might be of interest to you, including:

Basic Applications of Adlerian Psychology by Elizabeth A. Dewey (Coral Springs, FL: CMTI Press, 1978). Written in lay terms for the general public, this book describes the principles of Adlerian psychology as applied to relationships and self-understanding.

Children: The Challenge by Rudolph Dreikurs (NY: Dutton, 1987). This classic publication helps parents improve their relationships with their kids by spelling out the four mistaken goals of behavior, and why children choose to act in certain ways or misbehave. Also offers ideas on how parents can recognize their own response patterns and learn to respond more positively.

Final Report: U.S. Department of Health and Human Services/McKnight Foundation Task Force on Eating Disorders (Minneapolis: Search Institute, 1996). A summary of a report that grew out of a unique planning process initiated by the U.S. Public Health Services Office on Women's Health and the McKnight Foundation. In the process, scientists, clinicians, health-care professionals, eating disorder organizations, and all the agencies of the U.S. Public Health Services worked together to explore ways to start a campaign to prevent and treat eating disorders.

Growing Smart: What's Working for Girls in School, Executive Summary and Action Guide by Sunny Hansen, Joyce

Walker, and Barbara Flom (Washington, DC: American Association of University Women Educational Foundation, 1995). The AAUW Educational Foundation launched a major research initiative several years ago to investigate what girls experience in school. *Growing Smart* presents an overview of approaches that foster girls' achievement and healthy development.

PRIDE Questionnaire Report: 1995–96 National Summary/ Girls, United States, Grades 6–12 (Bowling Green, KY: Pride Surveys, 1996). Each year, PRIDE (National Parents' Resource Institute for Drug Education) conducts a nation-wide survey of drug use by junior and senior high school students and publishes the results. The published survey provides information on young peoples' use of drugs, alcohol, and cigarettes, and on school violence.

Reviving Ophelia: Saving the Selves of Adolescent Girls by Mary Pipher, Ph.D. (NY: Ballantine Books, 1994). This groundbreaking book explores issues affecting girls growing up in our society today, including divorce, depression, body image, sexuality, and violence. The author examines female adolescence and offers concrete suggestions to help girls build and maintain a strong sense of self.

SGR 4 Kids: The Surgeon General's Report for Kids About Smoking (Washington, DC: U.S. Government Printing Office, 1994). A report written by and for kids that offers insights for adults as well. Provides information on how young people across the nation feel about smoking, shares an interview with the Surgeon General by young people, and identifies companies that promote cigarettes to kids.

The Troubled Journey: A Profile of 6th–12th Grade Youth by Peter L. Benson, Ph.D. (Minneapolis: Search Institute, 1991). Based on a nationwide survey of over 46,000 students in grades 6–12, this report identifies the developmental assets and deficits that influence students' ability to make positive choices in their lives. Includes recommendations for families, schools, churches, and communities to help youth build assets.

Index

About the Authors

Gladys Folkers, M.A. is a psychotherapist and educator who provides individual therapy to adolescents; approximately 80 percent of clients she sees in her private practice are adolescent girls. She also facilitates a variety of support groups for adolescent girls, which focus on issues including chemical use, relationship problems, sexuality, abuse, and self-esteem. Gladys is also a parent educator and a consultant for professionals who work with adolescents, and a crisis intervention counselor in several middle school and alternative school programs. Her public speaking and workshop/ training presentations include topics such as parenting teens, living with an adolescent daughter, adolescent depression, bringing out the best in your children, and working with adolescents.

Jeanne Engelmann is an author and freelance writer. She focuses much of her nonfiction writing on topics such as chemical dependency, women, and adolescents. Because of her experience with chemical dependency as a teenager, Jeanne brings a personal sense of urgency to the discussion of how girls can best navigate oftentimes perilous adolescent waters. She also writes fiction for middle grade and young adult readers.

Other Books from Free Spirit Publishing

Totally Private and Personal: Journaling Ideas for Girls and Young Women

by Jessica Wilber

Written by a fourteen-year-old, this book offers personal insights, experiences, and guidance—journaling tips and suggestions, advice about being a girl, things to do, and more. Serious and funny, upbeat and down-to-earth. Ages 11–16.

$8.95; 168 pp.; softcover, 5 1/8" x 7 3/8", $8.95

Fighting Invisible Tigers: A Stress Management Guide for Teens

by Earl Hipp

Advice for coping with stress, being assertive, building supportive relationships, taking risks, making decisions, staying healthy, dealing with fears and misconceptions, recognizing perfectionism, and more. Ages 11 and up.

$10.95; 160 pp.; illust.; softcover; 6" x 9"

Making the Most of Today: Daily Readings for Young People on Self-Awareness, Creativity, and Self-Esteem

by Pamela Espeland and Rosemary Wallner

Quotes from figures including Eeyore, Mariah Carey, and Dr. Martin Luther King, Jr., guide young people through a year of positive thinking, problem-solving, and practical lifeskills. Ages 11 and up.

$8.95; 392 pp.; softcover; 4" x 7"

To place an order or to request a copy of our free catalog, please write or call:

Free Spirit Publishing Inc.

400 First Avenue North, Suite 616
Minneapolis, MN 55401-1730
Toll-free (800)735-7323, Fax (612)337-5050
E-mail: help4kids@freespirit.com